# CAREERS IN
# TELEVISION

# CAREERS IN TELEVISION

By
*JEANNE NAGLE*

The Rosen Publishing Group, Inc.
New York

Published in 2001 by The Rosen Publishing Group, Inc.
29 East 21st Street, New York, NY 10010

First Edition

*Cover photo ©John Coletti/Pictor*

**Library of Congress Cataloging-in-Publication Data**

Nagle, Jeanne
    Careers in television / by Jeanne Nagle — 1st ed.
       p. cm. — (Careers)
    Includes bibliographical references and index.
    ISBN 0-8239-3187-0 (lib. bdg.)
    1. Television—Vocational guidance—Juvenile literature. I. Title.
II. Careers (Rosen Publishing Group)
    PN1992.55 .N24  2000
    791.45'02'93—dc21                    00-009849

*Manufactured in the United States of America*

# About the Author

Jeanne Nagle is a freelance writer and the copy editor of a weekly business newspaper in upstate New York, where she makes her home.

# Contents

# Introduction

Television—it's entertaining. If it wasn't, why would we watch so much of it? A whopping 98 percent of households own at least one television, and those sets are turned on for an average of seven hours a day. It has been estimated that an individual in this country actively watches at least four hours of television a day; that's about twenty-eight hours a week. Experts say that is more time than is spent reading books or going to the movies.

Television—it's informational. By running news shows, documentaries, travel programs, and the like, television can teach us about different cultures, keep us aware of current events, take us places we might never even have heard of before, and allow us to explore things we might never have considered.

Television—it's powerful. Like other media, television can sway public opinion and can influence what we think and how we feel. Its combination of pictures and words, as well as its sense of immediacy, can challenge and help to change policy and laws, and can open up important issues for debate.

So, you've given it some thought and you've decided that working in television would make for a pretty interesting career. Fair enough, but there are still a few things you need to consider before you move ahead with your plan.

Do you want to work in news or entertainment? Do you want to inform people or amuse them? Maybe you'd like to do a little of both?

Do you want to work in front of the camera or behind it? Maybe even work the camera itself? What interests you most: being part of a creative team, working on the business end, or maybe taking part in the more technical side?

Keep in mind that the kind of job in television you choose, and how successful you would like to be at that job, can affect not only the size of the paycheck you take home but also where that home will be. There are opportunities everywhere to work in television, from small towns to large cities. However, the larger markets generally allow more opportunity for advancement. Also, you might need to live in a specific location to find certain kinds of work. For instance, if you want to be an actor in a television series or a scriptwriter, you may need to live in Los Angeles.

This book describes a number of the most popular jobs in television, including the duties of and skills required for each position, the experience and/or education needed to get started in each, and rough estimates of salaries. The information in these pages should help you decide if a career in television is right for you.

# *An Overview*

Chances are that when you start applying for work in television, you will be judged mainly on your experience, attitude, appearance, and skills. Still, general knowledge of the industry is also important.

Being aware of the history of television, how job positions in the television industry are categorized, how things operate, and what current trends are hot will make you a well-rounded candidate. Such knowledge also shows that you have an interest in television as a whole, and are not just interested in bringing home a paycheck in a glamorous profession.

Knowing a little background information about the field will also make you feel more confident and sound more professional. When an employer asks why you want a job in television, you won't have to rely on answers like, "I watch a lot of television and I think it's cool." With this in mind, here is an overview of the television industry.

## A BRIEF HISTORY OF TELEVISION

Because most of us grew up with television as a central part of our lives, it is easy to think that it has been around forever. The truth is that television—at least the technology for it—is only about seventy years old. Broadcast television, which is what we watch today, is even younger.

The bulk of technology that made television possible was being developed around the same time that radio was popular, in the 1920s. Most of the experiments with television were done somewhat secretly because the people working on them also had a lot of money tied up in radio, and they didn't want the new "radio with pictures" to take profits away from that.

The first televisions were mechanical. They essentially consisted of a metal disc with holes punched in it through which light was shone. The filtered light was then transformed into electrical impulses. The picture that these mechanical television sets made, however, was not very clear.

In the late 1920s, the Great Depression put most television research on hold. At least one company, though, had enough money to continue experimenting and inventing. That company was RCA, which had made its riches in radio sales and from the profits of its radio network, the National Broadcasting Company (NBC). The company invested money not in mechanical television, but in a newer technology that produced a clearer picture. By 1932, the mechanical method was replaced by electronic television, which is the version we use today.

In America, a man named Philo T. Farnsworth was a pioneer in the development of electronic television. Farnsworth made many discoveries outside of the television industry, including work on microscopes, incubators, and an early version of the fax machine. He began diagramming and tinkering with prototypes for electronic television as a teenager on his family's farm in Utah, and he later incorporated information he had learned in college and in science magazines.

He even studied glassblowing so that he could perfect the cathode-ray tubes needed to make his version of television work.

Working with Vladimir Zworykin, who invented the television camera and the television viewing screen, Farnsworth helped to make electronic television a reality.

In the early 1930s, RCA, which fought with Farnsworth over the patents on his inventions, made a deal with the inventor that allowed the company to use his television technology. They worked to make television a commercial success.

By 1935, there were fewer than 4,000 electronic television sets in operation—not that there was much to watch, anyway. The experimental stations operated by the RCA network and its rival, CBS, aired very few shows, which usually ran half an hour or less. In fact, one of the first broadcasts in 1937 was seen mostly by a few hundred RCA employees and affiliated workers crammed into the Empire State Building. They watched just a few television sets that the company had arranged as a display.

NBC worked a few more years to make the quality of the picture even better before beginning to air regular programming. In 1939, NBC broadcast the opening ceremonies of the New York World's Fair. RCA also had a pavilion at the World's Fair dedicated to television, where television sets were sold. However, not many people could afford to buy even the cheapest model, which cost about $200.

It wasn't until after World War II that a sizable portion of the public started buying television sets and watching broadcasts. By 1948, approximately 250,000 households in America had a television tuned to one of four networks: NBC, CBS, ABC, and the Du Mont Television Network.

Today, almost every home in this country has at least one television set. Three of the four initial networks have survived, and they have been joined by many cable stations. Telecommunications satellites, the first of which was launched in 1962, make it possible for television transmissions to be broadcast and received virtually around the globe. Color television—which came on the scene in 1954 in America, even though scientists had been tinkering with the technology for it since the late 1920s—is now the norm. Inventions such as DVD and interactive television have further expanded the horizons of television production and viewing.

## COMMERCIAL AND NONCOMMERCIAL TELEVISION

Most of the broadcast television that we see today is what's known as commercial television. To support themselves, television stations must sell advertising time in which they run commercials during their programs. Advertisers use that time to run sales pitches, or commercials, for their products. That's why it is called commercial television. How much advertisers pay for time on the air depends on the popularity of the program during which the commercial will run, and what time of day the spot is shown.

Commercial revenue is important to the networks and the local stations with which they have agreements, which are called affiliates. There are some 600 to 700 network affiliates in the United States.

In addition, there are hundreds of independent stations across the country. Independent stations are owned by corporations and groups of businesspeople called conglomerates. These stations do not depend on network programming, the programs created and controlled by the major networks like FOX and CBS. Most of the independent stations have specialized programming, such as classic movies or programs that are purchased in syndication. (Syndication involves leasing programs to stations so that they can broadcast a program after its initial network run. For example, old episodes of *Friends* that are shown in the afternoon or late at night are being run in syndication.)

Noncommercial television does not rely on commercial revenue, but on the generosity of foundations, grants, businesses, the government, and individual donors. Basically, support comes from the public. That is why it is also known as public television.

The same kind of for-profit companies and organizations that buy airtime on commercial stations may make donations to public television stations to keep them running. Although noncommercial stations can publicly thank whoever makes donations, they are not allowed to run advertising like the commercial stations do. That is why you never see commercials on public television stations.

In 1969, the Public Broadcasting Service (PBS) was created to oversee the quality of programming and services available to noncommercial stations, which are known as member stations rather than affiliates. PBS, a nonprofit organization, helps its members with fundraising, engineering, and technological support, as well as with the creation and distribution of original programs.

In addition to its on-air programming, PBS is also involved in educational programming that is broadcast in classrooms. Approximately 500,000 students watched and learned from the service's telecourses during 1998 and 1999.

Despite not receiving huge sums of money from commercial revenue, noncommercial television has kept up with current technology. Among other initiatives, PBS has been a pioneer in the distribution of its programs via satellite, has sought to improve satellite audio and UHF transmitters, and was involved in the early stages of closed captioning for the hearing-impaired audience.

## CABLE TELEVISION

In the early days of television broadcasts, the signals—the way in which television is transmitted from the station to your home—could not reach very far, and only people who lived near the stations, which were typically located in the country's larger cities, could get clear reception.

This was a problem for John Walson, who owned an appliance store in the hills of Pennsylvania. He couldn't convince folks to buy televisions from him because they couldn't get a clean picture or good sound.

Walson's solution was to stick an antenna on a tall pole on top of a mountain outside his town, which would attract the signals being sent from stations far away. He then set up two other antenna wires, which brought the signal down to his store. From there, using coaxial cable and homemade amplifiers, he sent out transmissions to customers' homes through antennas connected to their television sets.

A few years later, in the 1950s, a man named Milton Shapp refined Walson's technology and designed a master antenna that could be used by all televisions in a given building. Robert Tarleton took that one step further and created a system that could work for a whole town.

Eventually, inventors improved on this technology and developed systems that enabled signals to be brought in from locations all over the country and around the world, not just from the nearest big city.

The potential of cable television reached a big turning point in the early 1970s with the introduction of Home Box Office (HBO). HBO was the first service to use a satellite to distribute its programming. Using this technology HBO was able to send its signal much farther while still maintaining quality reception. This allowed HBO to reach many more markets, or areas of distribution, than the old technology would have allowed.

Unlike network television, cable service is not free. Those who want to see the programming offered on cable television pay a monthly fee to their local service provider.

## Programming
Programming involves deciding which television programs the public sees, which day of the week and what time of day they are on, and how long they stay on the air.

The primary goal for those who work in commercial television is to win the highest ratings, which means getting the most viewers to watch the programs on their station or network. The more people who see a show, the more people there are who also see the commercials that air during the show. It is hoped that many of those people will buy the products advertised. That's good for the people selling the products, but it is also good for the television executives. If a commercial works well, then networks and stations can charge more for the airtime and/or get the advertiser to buy more time, both strategies that bring in more money.

To track the success of programming, there must be research into public opinion. In what is called a screening, programming executives invite people to watch the new shows stations plan to air. Then the executives ask the members of that sample audience what they like and dislike about the show.

Another method of research that programming executives use is to electronically monitor which shows particular households watch. This helps them to figure out which shows are popular and which are duds. The company most often associated with this type of monitoring is the A.C. Nielsen Company. It installs monitors on televisions in certain households and collects data regarding which shows are being watched. Using this information, the company creates the Nielsen ratings, which are taken very seriously by television professionals.

Programming is like a game network executives play, in which they try to figure out what kinds of shows the public wants, and then place those shows in the time slots in which they will get the highest ratings possible. This often involves a lot of juggling of shows and replacement of some poorly rated programs midseason.

Television programming generally falls into one of two categories: entertainment or news. Entertainment is designed to amuse the audience. With commercial stations, entertainment programming includes situation comedies (which are called sitcoms), dramas, documentaries, nature shows, game shows, sports, and made-for-television movies.

News programs can be local, produced by affiliates of different sizes in different cities, or national. You may have heard the national news referred to as the network news. The three big commercial networks in

America that broadcast nightly news are ABC, CBS, and NBC.

Although entertainment and news are two distinct categories, there is a certain amount of overlap to them as well. For instance, talk shows and the newsmagazine shows, such as *20/20* or *Dateline*, often contain elements of both entertainment and news. These shows report as a news show would on topics of concern or interest to viewers, but they frequently do so in an entertaining or dramatic way.

Public television focuses its programming on education and the arts. For example, it broadcasts a lot of educational shows for children—like *Sesame Street*—documentaries, nature shows, symphony concerts, and the like. In general, public television shows tend toward the academic and away from the sensationalism typically found on the commercial networks.

Commercial television networks produce some programs on their own, particularly news programs. Entertainment programs, however, are overseen by network executives and created by people in Hollywood, New York, and other big cities. These people put together and videotape or film the programs that air on commercial television.

Noncommercial television relies heavily on a National Program Service that PBS offers to its stations. Sources for programs include the member stations themselves, producers who are not affiliated with the networks, and various other independent sources.

## REGULATIONS

Television is regulated by the Federal Communications Commission (FCC), which also regulates other types of electronic communication, such as interstate telephone and amateur radio services. The commission's primary responsibility regarding television is to enforce the laws set forth by the Communications Act of 1934, which was designed to make sure commercial television stations "operate in the public interest, convenience, and necessity."

The commission is made up of seven members who are appointed by the president of the United States. Each member serves for a term of seven years. Together, they assign broadcast frequencies, grant and revoke broadcast licenses, and make sure that no person owns so many stations that he or she has a monopoly in any particular viewing area or market.

The FCC does not regulate television networks, just individual stations. For example, the commission does not determine which programs get aired or the content of those programs, but it is involved in any private disputes between individual stations. As a federal agency, the FCC cannot make any regulations without first getting input from the public. The commission sends out an explanation of the proposed new rule, then waits until the public has had time to comment on it before any new regulations go into effect.

## JOBS IN TELEVISION

When embarking on a particular career in television, you should have a plan of action. But first you need to weigh all the possible opportunities and decide what type of job would suit you best.

One of the first decisions you should make concerns whether you would prefer working in television news or entertainment programming.

News broadcasts stick to the facts, reporting on current events and, on local stations, weather and sports. Network news operations, which bring us the nightly newscasts seen across the country, are based in New York City.

Entertainment television involves programs like sitcoms, dramas, made-for-television movies, and the like. These shows are generally fiction, and they are made strictly for the audience's enjoyment. Operations for the entertainment side of television are typically centered in the Los Angeles area.

Another choice you will need to consider is whether you would like to work in front of the camera or behind the scenes.

We are most familiar with jobs in which people work in front of the camera because they are the faces of television. The people who do these jobs—including actors, news anchors, game show hosts, and talk show hosts—sometimes become celebrities.

But there are many other jobs that are crucial to getting the programming into homes around the country. Behind-the-scenes personnel include management, administrative personnel who make sure the business end runs smoothly; creative people, such as writers; those who oversee content, such as editors; and the technicians who make sure that all of the machinery works properly.

Whether they work in front of the camera or behind it, the people who work in television are involved in at least one of three distinct stages of a program: preproduction, production, and postproduction.

Preproduction refers to the time before a television show airs. The people in these positions do the legwork and prepare for what comes on to your screen. Writers are a good example of preproduction personnel.

Production refers to the actual process of filming or videotaping something, or, in the case of a live show, the time during which it is being broadcast. Technicians who work the cameras, lights, and control boards, and the on-camera talent such as actors and news anchors, are the main players during production.

Postproduction is the area dominated mainly by technicians, who put the finishing touches on the work and clean up all the rough spots. Rerecording artists and producers are just two examples of people who work in this area.

There also are some jobs, such as directing and producing, that cross all of the boundaries and are involved in each step of production. The following chapters will give you more information that will help you to choose which job is right for you.

# 2

# On-Air Jobs

Nothing could be more glamorous than being on television and having thousands—even millions—of people recognize you and treat you as if you are special. You can make pretty good money, too.

Those are certainly the perks of having a job in front of the television camera. Yet these positions also demand a lot of hard work and preparation.

## ACTORS

So, you want to be a star. Well, it just might happen for you the way it did for your favorite television actors. However, for every person who makes it to the big time, there are plenty of actors who do not. Becoming an actor who works in television is difficult, but it is not impossible.

Everybody knows that actors act. They entertain audiences by pretending to be different people and enacting an interesting story.

One of the top skills for actors is creativity. They must play a part and make that character believable. Actors also have to be versatile. One day an actor may be in a sitcom, and the next he or she may appear in a dramatic television movie.

Generally, actors are not shy, at least not while they are in front of the camera. They typically are confident individuals and are more than a little extroverted.

They need to have a good memory to learn their lines and be able to improvise. They must also work well with others because a lot of acting requires interacting with fellow actors and directors.

While it is important that actors follow their instincts, they must also be able to follow directions. They need to listen to and incorporate into their performance the instructions of the director.

Actors must photograph well, although that does not mean that they all must be beautiful or handsome. There are plenty of roles for people of different physical types and looks, although being pleasing to the eye is certainly a plus in this field.

## What to Expect

One of the first things a beginning television actor should do is hire an agent to help him or her find work. An agent's job is to talk to the people, called casting directors, who hire actors for shows. Agents arrange for the actors they represent to try out, or audition, for parts.

Actors who can't find an agent who is interested in representing them or who feel they can make it on their own spend a lot of their time and energy just trying to develop the connections they need to get auditions. Many key people in television casting will not even consider a person who is not represented by an agent or manager.

As you've probably heard hundreds of times before, a career as an actor can be quite a roller-coaster ride. Unless he or she is hired to star in a regular series, an actor may be working one day and then unemployed for weeks or months after that. Even a steady job in a series is no guarantee of success because the show could be canceled at any time.

Also, many actors, particularly those just starting out, don't have much of a choice about which parts they play. Oftentimes, they have to take what they can get. They audition for and take any role that is offered them because they know that the more experience they have, the better they look to the people who do the hiring. Even those who have been at it for a while are not above taking a small part if it means they can work.

Aside from being a star, there are other levels to acting, such as guest starring and playing supporting roles. Some jobs do not even require the actor to speak scripted lines.

Actors can also find work in commercials. In fact, many famous actors began their careers in this way, and some continue to use their image or voice to sell products even after they have become famous.

To further their careers and protect their interests, actors work hand-in-hand with unions. These are groups of people in the same profession who gather together to give themselves strength when it comes to ensuring things like fair pay and safe working conditions. For television actors, the main unions are the Screen Actors Guild (SAG) and the American Federation of Television and Radio Artists (AFTRA).

Lots of people want to be actors, but not everybody is good at it. Even those who have some talent may not make a living from acting because of the sheer number of people who also have talent and are trying to make it.

The competition from other actors is tough enough, but in this profession you may also have to fight the Hollywood establishment. Executives generally don't want to work with you unless you are established. Actors are judged on how marketable they are at the moment, not how successful they have been in the past or might be in the future.

How long a person can make a living at being an actor depends on talent, versatility, and how hard he or she works at it. But age can be a factor. Executives know that people between the ages of twenty and forty are those most likely to be influenced by the ads that appear during shows. They are also the people who have the buying power to act on that influence. So executives create shows that people in that age bracket can relate to, which generally means they feature characters of the same age group.

While some 30 percent of those who try to be actors give up after the first few years, and the competition in the field is tough, there are still a number of good acting jobs to be had. New series are produced all the time, and with growing cable, satellite, and foreign distribution markets, the demand for acting talent shouldn't diminish anytime soon.

### Experience

You can take classes in acting, but the only way to get useful experience as an actor is to act. Virtually every school has a drama department or some group that puts on plays. You should join yours. It doesn't matter if you win the lead or a small part in the chorus of a musical, or even if you decide merely to join the stage crew and help build sets and move the scenery. Any connection to the theater will teach you about the world of acting.

There are things you can do outside of school, too. You can join a community theater group, or volunteer at your local cable access station for work behind or in front of the camera.

Be creative. Think up unconventional ways to gain experience. For instance, have you ever considered volunteering to read stories at your local kindergarten, day care center, or library? This is a good way to practice delivering lines, as well as using and developing different voices. Acting out a short scene or doing a stand-up comedy act at a local talent show or open-mike night will also give you experience performing in front of a crowd.

## Education

Many people who want to act take drama and theater classes, either informally or in high school and college. Some colleges and universities, such as Juilliard and the University of California at Los Angeles, have entire programs devoted to the craft. At these institutions, one can earn a bachelor of fine arts degree or even a master of fine arts degree in theater or dramatic arts.

Students pursuing this goal take lots of classes where they get to perform. In addition, college courses for a degree in drama include subjects such as speech, movement, dramatic literature (which involves reading and studying plays), and the history of drama. Theater-related arts such as playwriting and directing may also be offered.

In addition to taking classes in theater and the study and performance of plays, some actors also take classes to learn specialized skills. For instance, some might learn fencing or how to stage a realistic fight scene. Plenty of actors concentrate heavily on singing and dancing to make themselves more well rounded and able to take on a wider variety of roles.

In this atmosphere, new actors can practice and see if they have what it takes. Of course, some veteran actors also take classes to brush up on their skills and keep their talent fresh.

Though training such as this is highly recommended, it is not a prerequisite to enter the field. In essence, actors need to be experts in human nature. You can "study" acting by paying close attention to the people around you. Examine how different people gesture, speak, and react to situations.

Actors also need to learn from their experiences. If they have been successful with one part, they should study their performance to see what they did right. Likewise, if they feel they have flopped in a role, they should analyze that to make sure they don't make the same mistakes over and over again.

## Salary

The rates at which actors are paid are determined by bargaining agreements between those who produce television programming and the actors' unions. Considerations such as how many hours and days an actor works and whether he or she has any lines to speak set the pay scale.

These days, actors with a nonstarring speaking part in a television series or movie generally earn several hundred or a few thousand dollars a day. That seems like good money, until you remember that acting jobs can be few and far between. Minimum annual salary estimates for actors range from as low as $5,000 to a high of $35,000.

Of course, famous actors make much more than that. Stars of popular shows can make millions each year. Keep in mind that these salaries are the exception. Most actors' incomes fall somewhere in the minimum range listed previously, or perhaps in a middle range that is somewhat higher but not nearly as much as a star makes.

## REPORTERS

Reporters are not just faces that deliver a story. They have to conduct research, interview people, and write. They need to be able to write a news story so that it contains all the important facts, is not too long, and is easy to understand, even if the subject matter is very complex.

In small markets, a reporter may be asked to do everything. This includes not only the usual research, interviews, writing, and presentation, but possibly shooting and editing their own video as well.

A reporter is always on the alert, looking for stories and chasing down leads. The smaller the market, the smaller the staff, which means reporters are pulling double duty and are even more on the go than their counterparts in larger markets.

To get even an entry-level job, reporters will most likely need to show a prospective employer a demo tape. This is a videotaped portfolio, a compilation of stories the reporter has researched, written, interviewed for, and delivered on camera.

### Experience

If you want to become a reporter, you will need to gain experience in many disciplines. You will need to learn how to come up with story ideas, gather information, conduct interviews, write stories that you research, and shoot and edit your video footage.

Reporters often get experience by working with a college or university television station. You can also start getting this experience in high school, even if there is no campus television station. Writing for a school newspaper or working at a student-run radio station teaches you the basics of reporting: research, writing, and presentation of the news. If there is no television station at your school and you have your heart set on being on television, then volunteer to host a show on your local cable access network or apply for an internship.

Reporters should not be afraid to accept jobs at stations in smaller markets. While these positions do not pay as much as the larger networks, and their exposure is limited, they are a terrific place to learn the ropes and gain experience.

Because small stations have small staffs, each person usually carries out many different tasks. For example, a reporter at a small station may research, develop, and shoot footage for his or her story while a reporter at a large network may only stand in front of the camera and report on a story that someone else created. By working at a small station, you will become more well-rounded, be able to be more creative, and gain valuable experience that will be useful when you apply for your big network position.

### Education

Even though heavy emphasis is placed on practical experience, a bachelor's degree in journalism is the minimum requirement to get hired by the majority of broadcasting stations in America. Typical undergraduate level classes in broadcast journalism include writing and reporting, video production and presentation, and the ethics of journalism. Students also learn about the tools of the trade, including cameras, lights, and sound equipment.

Additionally, in order to remain competitive, some reporters will get an advanced degree in broadcast journalism. Experts are divided about how important going to graduate school is for an aspiring journalist. Some say it won't teach you anything you can't learn as an undergraduate or by practical experience. Others point out that a graduate degree looks good on your résumé and could even bring a higher starting salary.

No matter what kind or level of education you decide to get, the important thing is to take courses that give you practice in writing. Many news directors, who do the hiring for reporting positions, complain that not enough reporters have the skill to write a clean, understandable story. If you can master this skill, you have a better shot at winning a reporting job.

## Salary and Other Compensation

This is not the field in which you are going to get rich right away. Typical starting salaries for television reporters can start as low as $12,000, but the average is somewhere in the low twenties.

The actual pay rate depends on the size and location of the market. The larger the market, the better the pay is likely to be. Once a reporter moves up into one of the top twenty-five markets in the United States, the average pay can range from $50,000 to upward of $150,000, depending on the amount of experience you have. Reporters who choose to stay in a smaller or midsize market can still bump up into a higher pay bracket by working to become anchors.

## ANCHORS

News anchors, also referred to as newscasters or news analysts, are some of the most visible people in television news. They are the people with whom the public most identifies a station or a particular news program.

An anchor's job is to make sure newscasts flow from one segment to the next as smoothly as possible. They do this by presenting stories themselves and by introducing the work of others, whether it is their fellow anchors or reporters.

On national newscasts, anchors such as Dan Rather and Tom Brokaw work alone. Many local stations, even ones in larger cities like Chicago and New York, typically have a pair of news anchors, usually a man and a woman. In addition, local stations or affiliates will feature weathercasters and sportscasters.

Weathercasters, or meteorologists, collect data about the weather from sources around their area and across the nation. Many rely on their station's resources to get accurate local information. This information can be very technical, so part of a meteorologist's job is to make it easy to understand.

Sportscasters perform the same kinds of tasks as news anchors, only they concentrate on the world of sports. They cover everything from national championships in pro sports to weekly high school contests.

One of the skills needed to make a career as a television anchor is looks. These people must be neat and professional in appearance. Being well groomed for an anchor means wearing makeup and using hair styling products—for both men and women. These professionals also need to photograph well and be comfortable in front of the camera.

This does not mean that to make it as a television anchor you have to be a former model. "I'm not saying I hire only beautiful people," says one man who hires for a television station, "because that would not be true. In fact you can be too pretty for television. But it certainly is a visual medium, and you want to see somebody who's presentable."

Because television is a visual medium, many people think that looks are the most important qualification for making it in the field. This is not so. Remember, people not only watch television, they listen to it as well. Using improper English, having an unpleasant-sounding voice or a very strong accent, or not being able to speak smoothly can be a distraction because such traits can make the anchor difficult to understand and frustrating to listen to. Anchors also must be sure that they do not sound stiff, as if they are just reading from cue cards or off a sheet of paper. Anchors need to sound like they are having a personal conversation with the viewer. Sometimes anchors need help from speech or diction coaches so that they can present the news in a clear voice.

More than that, anchors need to be good community members. The public needs to trust a news anchor, to believe that the news he or she is delivering is accurate and trustworthy. If an anchor misbehaves in public or does not come across as very likable, viewers are not going to think that person is trustworthy, and they won't watch his or her newscast.

## What to Expect

It is not a wise idea to plan on immediately becoming a television news anchor. Most of the people who are in those positions had to work their way up, usually by being reporters for a number of years. You should expect to take the same route.

Depending on the size of the station and the number of news broadcasts it has, a station could have several anchors or teams of anchors. Weekdays during the main broadcast before the network news—which usually runs either at 5:00 or 6:00 PM—and the broadcast after prime-time commercial programming—at 10:00 or 11:00 PM—belong to the main or "star" anchors at a station. Other newscasts, including those on the weekends, are the domain of what could be called regular anchors.

## Experience

Anchors are usually reporters who have worked hard to show that they have what it takes to run the entire news program. They generally start out their work as anchors in small markets, perhaps doing an early-morning show for a local station or filling in on the weekends. Like reporters, anyone who wants to become an anchor will have to produce a demo tape, which is a videotape of them working a newscast.

One former sportscaster estimates that he put together as many as 130 stories as an intern, many of which made it on air. More important, after working on that many stories, he felt he had enough good material to put together an audition tape, which he shopped around, or tried to sell, to a few stations in the hope of getting a full-time sportscasting job.

## Education

Most broadcast stations prefer to hire anchors with at least a bachelor's degree, preferably one in journalism. The stations in large cities would also like something to back that up, such as a minor in economics, political science, or business.

When you enroll in college to study journalism, you can expect most of your classes to be general liberal arts courses. The journalism classes will cover topics such as mass media, the history of journalism, basic reporting and copyediting skills, and journalism law and ethics. As a future broadcast journalist, you will also be required to take courses in television newscasting and production. It is possible to continue in school and get either a master's degree or doctorate in journalism as well.

You don't have to wait until college to start learning to be an anchor, however. Some high school courses, such as English, creative writing, history, and speech, are good ways to start developing the skills and knowledge that will help you to become a good anchor. The ability to read, write, and speak a language other than English are also great skills to have.

Perhaps most important, television news employers are looking for candidates who have practical training. Most stations will not consider someone for an anchor position until he or she has a minimum of three to five years' experience as a reporter.

## Salary

Anchors, particularly main anchors, are some of the most highly paid professionals in television news. In midsize to large markets, they may even make more than those in management positions, such as news directors.

For a station's first team of anchors, or those who are in the prime-time spots, salaries can range from the middle to high twenties in small markets to close to $200,000 or $300,000 in large markets. It has been reported that some prime-time anchors in major metropolitan areas such as New York City and Los Angeles earn upward of $1 million a year.

Second-tier, or regular, news anchors make a good deal less. Starting salaries can be as low as the high teens but average around $22,000 in the smaller markets. The most highly paid regular anchors, found in the top twenty-five markets, can see salaries in the $150,000 range.

First-string sportscasters and weathercasters don't make quite as much as their anchor counterparts do, but it's close. The range for these jobs generally starts at about the same level in the smaller markets, but reaches only about $100,000 to $125,000 on the very high end of the scale.

# *3*

# *Behind the Scenes: Creative*

We all can recite the names of famous newscasters and actors, but other than a couple of well-known directors, how many of us can list the people who work behind the scenes in television?

There are any number of people who work behind the scenes in television who contribute as creatively as do the folks in front of the camera. This chapter discusses some of the more popular positions.

## DIRECTORS

Directors are the men and women in charge of television storytelling. Their job is to decide what goes into a television show or newscast and then decide what he or she thinks are the important points in that content. Directors also are in charge of finding the crew and talent who can put together a good show.

A news director oversees a television newsroom. One man in this position likens his job to that of an editor at a newspaper. He decides which stories to cover and how they will be presented to the viewer. The news director is usually in charge of hiring and firing the staff who report to him or her, which includes anchors, reporters, and producers, among others.

Directors are involved with television production from the very beginning, when the planning and formation of the show take place, right through the broadcast.

In the case of filmed or videotaped work, they also take part in the postproduction editing process.

Directors have to be able to spot and hire talented people and work well with them. They need to know the ins and outs of working with people who may have fragile egos, such as actors and anchors. They also need to have knowledge about these people's craft in order to get them to perform at their best.

Organization is an important trait for directors. They are heavily involved in shooting schedules and are under strict deadlines.

Directors who work on television series or movies work with editors to put together the final version of a show. At this stage of the production, directors must make good use of their sense of pacing and structure, and put scenes together so they make sense and are entertaining.

News directors, because their shows are live, do not have the luxury of filming several takes and editing out mistakes. For the most part, news directors have to get it right the first time. Also, they must watch the clock very closely, making sure they don't go over or under the time that they are allotted.

Directors also need to be money-conscious. Entertainment shows, television movies, and news programs all are subject to budgets, and it is partly the responsibility of the director to make sure that productions don't cost more than they should. Directors also must balance the need to use money wisely with their artistic vision. A great idea might come to them, but if they don't have the financial resources to make it happen, then they may not be allowed to do it, or may have to be creative and find a less expensive way to put their idea into action.

## What to Expect

You aren't likely to get to be a director on a major television show or newscast without paying your dues first. You need to get work in the field, at any level.

Time spent in the business, even if you're not directing, is important because directors need to be knowledgeable about all of the components needed to create a television program, such as acting, camera work, and lighting. For this reason, many directors start out as production assistants (PAs) because they get to be involved in many different parts of television production. But being a PA is only one way to get started. Several successful directors began their television careers as actors, writers, or producers.

Some novice directors start out directing projects that are not created for television, such as industrial training films for companies, or local commercials. Not only will you have clips of your work to show prospective employers, but you get paid as well.

As a director, you shouldn't expect to have a normal work week. Directors work long hours. On average, they work more than sixty-five hours a week, and the time commitment can be much larger if you're involved with a big-budget project. Working round the clock is not the norm, but it can happen. Long days are only part of the picture for beginning directors, who must also deal with low pay and tons of pressure to prove themselves.

Directors on the entertainment side, particularly on commercial network shows and movies of the week, have at least one assistant to help them. Assistant directors perform some of the tasks of a director but mostly do the menial jobs the director doesn't have time for.

Not many news directors have an assistant news director. If they need backup, that usually becomes the job of an assignment editor or an executive producer. On the studio floor and on-site during live broadcasts, stage managers act as the director's representative, while news directors work from the control room or another nearby location.

### Experience

Think small when starting as a director. Offer to direct or help with directing a school or community-theater production. Take classes and put together amateur or student videos that you can use as examples of your work. You will need these samples, or clips, of your work when you interview for jobs.

One of the best ways to ensure that you get to direct is to come up with a project yourself. This includes mapping out the story and plot, writing the script, hiring the actors and technicians, and doing postproduction work such as editing in addition to directing.

Beginners who choose this route usually wind up paying for these projects out of their own pockets, and they have no guarantee that the work will ever get aired. Whether or not the project sells doesn't matter because at least it will act as a demo reel, which shows prospective employers what you can do.

### Education

Although it is not a requirement, many people who want to become directors go to film school. As a student, you will study the basics of media production, including video, writing, cinematography, editing, sound and production planning, as well as directing.

Students are also required to create at least one student film. This student film can serve as part of your directing portfolio.

## Salary

The salary of a television director in entertainment averages from $30,000 to $40,000 a year. Those starting out might earn only half that much, while experienced directors can take home $160,000 or more.

Although news directors are the bosses at a television news station, they don't necessarily get paid as much as the on-air talent. Typically, the average salary for those who run television newsrooms in the United States is around $50,000. That's more than the average anchor, but frequently less than a station's star anchor.

A lot also depends on the news director's experience, the size of the market and the size of the staff he or she oversees. In smaller markets, with smaller staffs, a news director might make about $30,000, whereas the same position at one of the top network affiliates— where the staff he or she oversees can number close to 100—might command more than $100,000.

Very few stations employ an assistant news director. For those positions that do exist, the salary ranges between $27,000 in the smaller markets and approximately $80,000 in the top markets.

## PRODUCERS

Producers oversee many of the components that go into creating a television program or newscast. They are responsible for everything from making sure writers and on-air talent do their jobs correctly to checking facts and making sure information is up-to-date. In the television newsroom, producers frequently write the newscast, adding to what the anchors and reporters may already have created. They also decide how the broadcast will be organized, determining the order and length of each of the segments. In entertainment, producers also are responsible for generating the money needed to create a program or movie.

Most producers start out as production assistants (PAs) who handle administrative and "gofer" tasks (like "going fer" coffee for the director). The work is very hard, the days can be long and grueling, and the pay is often relatively low. But if you stay with it, you are likely to move up. PAs often rise through the ranks to become production managers or assistant producers. Then, when they have paid their dues, they become producers and, someday, executive producers.

### Experience

Any work experience that shows you can juggle several tasks, handle stress, and keep people happy and productive is good experience for a production position.

As with so many jobs in all fields, internships are an important and useful way to gain experience. The connections made during an internship could lead to your first job in the business.

### Education and Training

It is particularly important that producers know the television business, but they also need to have plenty of general business savvy. That is why taking courses in business is important for those who want a job in production. Other useful classes include English, journalism, history, political science, psychology, and American studies.

Although it is not required, most producers earn at least a bachelor's degree. Some producers even receive advanced degrees—in journalism for news, or in film for the entertainment side—but this is not absolutely necessary.

## Salary

As with most other positions in local or affiliate television, producers' pay depends largely on the size of the market. Executive news producers in the largest markets make about $60,000—more than three times what those in small markets earn. Regular news producers earn closer to $40,000.

If a producer in television news wants to earn more, he or she generally moves ahead to become a news director. Producers on the entertainment end typically have higher salaries than their counterparts in news and can earn even more income if they become executive producers.

The money also may be better if a producer works for a network or a hit television program. Some producers are so highly respected that they end up working on several different programs, which, of course, raises their earning potential considerably.

## EDITORS

Editors are postproduction workers. They take all the parts of a product—pictures, sound, music, graphics—and blend them into a smooth, seamless story. In the newsroom, this person might be known as an electronic news gathering, or ENG, editor. This person takes the raw footage that was shot on location, stock footage, and tape taken from other sources and puts together a visual story that flows well.

Good editing is a combination of artistry and technical know-how. Like directors, editors must have a good sense of storytelling, so that they can weave all the parts of the filming into a coherent story. To accomplish this, they use technical skills such as cutting and splicing.

Specialized machinery and processes are a big part of an editor's workday. Editors operate computers, as well as equipment such as a Steenbeck, a Movieola, and a splicer.

Interpersonal skills and the ability to work as a team member are two more traits of a successful editor. Those in this field must work with sound editors and directors. Another benefit of interpersonal skills is the chance to form a lasting working relationship with directors and producers. If one of these professionals likes your editing work, he or she may keep hiring you on various projects for years to come.

Endurance is also key to success as an editor. Physical and mental toughness are important. An editor often puts in long hours, and most of the actual film or videotape editing is done alone, removed from all distractions, usually in a small room that is known as an editing bay.

Editors can find work in just about any town that has a television news station. The majority of jobs, however, are in New York City and Los Angeles.

### Experience

A number of editors start out as technicians or production assistants. Others may be lucky and land a job as an established editor's assistant.

It takes a while for an editor to earn his or her reputation. Some may toil for years as assistants, working on lower budget projects such as industrial or commercial videos before they find steady work as editors.

## Education

Editing is a technical trade that requires extensive training. Those who wish to enter the field generally have at least a bachelor's degree in electronic journalism from a liberal arts college or university, or from an accredited film school.

Courses focus on the history of film and television, broadcast journalism techniques, and, of course, basic editing skills. These classes offer not only the fundamentals of editing theory, but, because there is usually some kind of lab work attached to them, practical, hands-on experience as well.

Those who want to be editors should take advantage of their time in school and the connections made there to win internships with film and television production companies.

## Salary

The average starting salary for television editors is in the low twenties. The median range for an experienced editor is $40,000 to $50,000, although some can make upward of $70,000.

## WRITERS

Writers put together stories and create dialogue for on-camera talent. Those who write for entertainment television are commonly referred to as screenwriters. They may also go by other titles, such as story editor, story consultant, or even producer or co-executive producer. A television show these days typically is written by a team of writers headed by a chief writer, who is known as a showrunner. Showrunners create written material, but they are usually in charge of editing and revising the work done by the rest of the team.

A news writer's responsibilities go beyond putting words on a page. He or she must also do research and keep track of breaking news via wire services. Some news writers also have the responsibility of booking people for interviews or producing segments of a newscast.

There are also continuity writers. They are responsible for the copy used in local commercials, promotions, or public service announcements.

Writers should be detail-oriented and have a firm grasp of grammar and spelling. More than that, they need to put words together in an interesting way. Writers must write clear and concise copy, not letting their words get in the way of the story.

Television writers should be well read and, believe it or not, they should watch a lot of television. This gives them the chance to learn storytelling techniques and to see what works on television.

Writers also need to understand and be able to use the proper format for their scripts. Scripts contain character and scene descriptions, dialogue, and stage directions. All of these elements are put on the page in a particular way, using shorthand language common in the business. You will not be taken seriously, especially when you start out, if you submit a script that is not in the proper format.

Not only do you need to know how to write, but you need to know how to play the show business game. One screenwriter who works out of Los Angeles says that successful writers are easy to get along with, and know how to make themselves indispensable.

Attitude, in this instance, is everything. Make contacts and network. Make sure everyone knows how serious you are about a job as a television writer and don't give up the dream, no matter how tough and disappointing it all seems at first.

Television screenwriters have a lot of people to please. They are not writing only for themselves. Television writers need to have scripts that they can sell to network executives and that will make viewers want to watch. They need to put good writing into their scripts, but they must also consider the tastes and desires of the executives and the audience.

Staff writers may spend up to twelve hours at the office writing, and then be expected to write after-hours and on weekends to meet deadlines. There are plenty of rewrites, and writers may have to change dialog at the last minute.

Writers in television also can work on a freelance basis. These individuals, however, typically spend about half of their day calling around shopping, their ideas or scripts, instead of writing.

As a television screenwriter, you will need to work with an agent who can help you shop around your ideas. Usually, agents can make further inroads with executives than an unknown writer can.Like actors, writers are protected by unions, notably the Writer's Guild of America.

### Experience

The pros recommend taking every television and film class you can, even if they don't pertain directly to writing. As one writer put it: "A script isn't an end in itself. It's written to be produced, so the more you know about production, the better writer you'll be."

Another safe bet is to get a job as a script reader. It's a low-level job that pays about $30 for every script you read, but it gets you in the game. An extra advantage is that this type of work can offer you insight into what works and what doesn't. It can also familiarize you with the correct script format. Plus, you will have a built-in networking relationship with an executive who, because he or she likes you and the way you do your job, just might take a look at a script you have written.

Networking is crucial to gaining experience. As one experienced screenwriter put it: "The bottom line is there isn't a producer or exec I know who wouldn't rather buy from or hire a friend than an outsider, even if the outsider's work is a notch or two better. So your job as a new writer is to be the kind of person who can become that friend."

## Education

There are no formal education requirements to become a writer. However, many writers have at least a bachelor's degree—usually in English, creative writing, or journalism.

Internships are available at television newsrooms across the country. Chances are that you'll get some writing experience, particularly at smaller stations.

The colleges and universities with top-rated television and film schools, such as UCLA, USC, and NYU, all have excellent internship programs as well. As one insider said of these programs: "They have launched many a career."

## Salary and Other Compensation

The average yearly salary for broadcast television news writers is about $26,300. Successful staff writers for entertainment shows in Hollywood can earn much more. Speaking about those working in the entertainment side of commercial broadcasting, one television writer stated on his Web site: "Staff writers get about $2,500 a week to start, and that doesn't count any scripts you actually write. For those you get, depending on the nature of the series, between $6,000 (for animation) and $25,000 (for prime-time drama) an episode, or more."

# 4

# Behind the Scenes: Business and Administrative

Television stations and networks do not provide shows merely for our entertainment. They are in it to make money. Television is a business, and there are plenty of jobs that center on this aspect of the industry. This chapter explores a few careers you might want to look into.

## GENERAL MANAGERS

General managers (GMs) are the top executives at a television station. They oversee and coordinate the many different employees and departments. It is the general manager's job to make plans and set policies that are designed to improve the quality of the programs offered, and to make money for the station.

A general manager needs business knowledge and an overall understanding of how each department operates. This person has to be a leader and must have excellent interpersonal skills. The general manager has to be able to communicate his or her plan clearly and persuasively, but also must be willing to listen to those directly under his or her command. Self-confidence and the ability to stand behind decisions are important for these individuals, but so is flexibility.

General managers should possess planning and problem-solving skills, as well as the ability to analyze data taken from reports and charts. They should be well organized and good at meeting deadlines. They need to have experience and knowledge in many administrative and managerial tasks. A background that includes finance, human resources, computers, marketing, and general management is ideal for this position.

### What to Expect

It can be nice being at the top. As a general manager, you will have an office and a support staff. However, being the boss also has its pressures and problems. How well a general manager does his or her job is judged by the station's ratings, so if for any reason the viewing numbers fall, it is often the general manager who takes the flak for it. In order to make his or her station the best that it can be, a general manager frequently works long hours, including nights and weekends.

As chief representatives of their stations, general managers often need to meet with advertisers, corporate executives, government officials (often from the FCC), and others in the television business. This means a lot of traveling to attend meetings and industry conferences.

### Experience

Many times a station will hire someone who has already worked as a general manager to take the helm of the operation. However, hiring from staff already at the station happens as well. Experienced managers in other departments who have shown they have strong leadership and decision-making skills stand the best chance of becoming general managers. Therefore, getting a job at a station—in any capacity—and working hard to prove you are capable is the best experience you can have for this position.

Acting as the station manager for your high school or college radio or television station is also good experience, as is being editor of the school yearbook or newspaper. Basically, any experience that you can get running an organization, including managing staff and overseeing a budget, will contribute to your chances of eventually becoming a general manager.

### Education and Training

Many general managers have a bachelor's degree in liberal arts or accounting. Many go on to earn a master's degree in business administration (MBA).

Management techniques can change, as can the way things run in the television industry. A general manager's skills must keep pace with new regulations and sudden waves of mergers and acquisitions. A general manager who wants to keep his or her job needs to stay current on the issues and legislation that affect the industry.

In addition to formal education, there also are business and managerial seminars and workshops that general managers can attend to sharpen their skills. These programs are usually sponsored by trade associations and groups familiar with the television industry. A side benefit is that they allow general managers to network and make contacts that may turn out to be useful later, as well as find out what rival stations are doing.

## Salary

General manager is one of the most highly paid positions at a television station. However, salary levels generally depend on the size of the market and the station. For instance, general managers of stations in the top markets such as Los Angeles, Chicago, and New York City get paid more than the GM of a station in a small town.

As a general manager, you can probably expect to make at least $35,000 to $40,000. The larger the market, the bigger the paycheck. It is not uncommon for general managers in big-city markets to see salaries of around $90,000 and into the six-digit range.

## PROGRAM DIRECTORS

The main responsibility of a program director is to arrange for shows to be broadcast on his or her station and set up the on-air schedule. On the local end, it's a bit of a juggling act, because he or she deals with input from several different sources. Program directors at local stations need to incorporate local programming with what syndicators, independent producers, and studios try to sell them, as well as feeds from the network, if they are an affiliate station. (Feeds are the programming signals that local affiliates tap into so that they can broadcast programs that the major networks air.)

The networks, which provide the feeds, have groups called affiliate relations teams. These teams work closely with the local program directors and their staffs, keeping them informed about what the network is doing. For instance, they detail which programs are being canceled or changing to a different time slot, how commercials should be set up and run during breaks in the network shows, and which new shows are being added to the schedule.

Other items a program director might take care of, depending on the market and station for which the director works, include dealing with the FCC and renewing the station's license; negotiating contracts with unions; and making sure that the station has a good relationship with viewers, the network, and independent producers. Some program directors are even in charge of cracking down on viewers who are illegally getting a network signal from an affiliate somewhere else.

There is a lot of paperwork involved when you are a program director. You have to file many reports, including quarterly reports to the FCC that prove that your station is abiding by all of the commission's rules. These reports can include anything from the number and type of public service announcements you air to the number of station tours given to local schoolchildren.

In addition, a program director usually has to issue reports on whether the station's programming meets the needs of the community. To accomplish this, he or she must first speak with members of the community and ask them what issues are of concern. Then the program director checks to make sure the station has produced and aired programming that covers those concerns.

The public gives feedback in other ways as well. If they are unhappy about some programming issue, they will call, write, or send e-mail messages to complain. Part of a program director's job is responding to complaints and questions asked by viewers.

This interaction with members of the community is one reason why program directors need to have good communication and interpersonal skills. In addition to dealing with the public, they also work closely with most of the departments within their station. The people they work with most include the network team members, producers and studio reps, the directors at the station, and, if the station is in a large enough market and there is enough money in the budget for one, a programming assistant.

Program directors also need to have sales and marketing savvy. As part of the management team, they have to be aware of what other departments do and be sensitive to the needs and duties of their coworkers. To succeed, it is vital that program directors be aware of programming trends and what the competition in their market is doing.

Although the typical workweek is forty to fifty hours long, the hours a program director works can increase if there is extra paperwork or if something goes wrong. He or she could get a phone call late at night because taped programs have been erased or are missing, or could be asked to work weekends because of a technical glitch. These instances are not common, but they do happen.

If you decide to become a program director, you may have to do a bit of homework to find a job. Major studios are buying more and more networks, and there are communications mergers and a general consolidation of services for large geographical areas, where one regional person does the work for several area stations. The result is that fewer program director positions are becoming available. In fact, in some cities these jobs are being phased out altogether.

### Experience

One of the best ways to get experience as a program director is to work your way up the ladder at a local station. Working in the sales department is a good place to start, as is working in traffic, which is where a lot of work that is similar to what a program director does gets handled. Those who work in traffic process the orders for commercials that the sales reps take. Traffic workers place the commercials into the right time slot and decide things like which particular ad for a client they are going to run and how often, in order to meet the contract the company has signed. They also make sure that the filmed or videotaped commercial is ready for the engineer to put on the air.

Because there is a lot of interaction with the public, those who wish to become a program director should join a nonprofit organization in their area and do some volunteer work in the community. This helps get you in touch with the needs and wants of community members so that you can program shows that better serve them.

### Education and Training

Continuing your education past high school is not necessarily required to become a program director, but it is still a good idea. Colleges and universities with a solid liberal arts program are the best bet because, among other things, they concentrate on developing your reading and writing skills. Some kind of television production classes, and maybe a film course or two, will help you understand how a station works and will sharpen your sense of what makes a television show good.

Internships are highly recommended for this field. It doesn't even have to be an internship in programming. An internship in production, creative services, sales, or even in the news department will help. Any of these can give you an appreciation for what other people at the station are going through and how, when you become a program director, you can work best with them.

## Salary

Pay for program directors can run anywhere from $20,000 in a small market to $150,000 or more in a top market. Regardless of the market size, beginners usually get the low end of whatever salary range the station offers.

## PRODUCTION MANAGERS

Production managers work as part of the production team. Usually answering only to producers and directors, they are in charge of many aspects of television production, particularly the business side. They supervise other members of the production team as well.

Even though they are called production managers, it is during pre- and postproduction that most of their work is done. These professionals help to get television programs up and running, and wrap up loose ends after filming is completed.

One of a production manager's primary responsibilities is to help manage the budget of a television show, which includes getting the best possible price on equipment, locations and staff. They also do some of the hiring; they are responsible for signing on production assistants and administrative help, and along with producers and directors, they have a hand in hiring technical crew members. Because they keep watch over the budget, some production managers also help negotiate actors' contracts and scout for locations.

A working knowledge of the many aspects of television production is essential to this job. Production managers must be familiar with each department within the television industry, since they will be interacting on some level with each. They also need to know what it is going to take to make the different departments run smoothly and efficiently, as this keeps costs to a minimum.

Production managers need to be well organized and able to prioritize. They need to be good at working with both people and numbers. They have to be able to deal with pressure because they not only have to work on deadline, but they have to balance the books to the satisfaction of a lot of other people, including producers, directors, and network executives. Production managers need to communicate clearly and assertively, as they are in charge of so much of the production. They also need to be able to delegate responsibilities and motivate others to do their jobs properly.

There is a lot of equipment involved in being a production manager. In addition to knowing the basics about the technical equipment they may be ordering, production managers need to be very comfortable with everyday business technology, such as word processors, cell phones, and calculators.

Teamwork is very important in television production. This means that production managers have a lot of contact with people from all parts of a television production team, including actors and crew members. They also deal with outside vendors who sell or lease the equipment and merchandise necessary to tape a television show. Being a production manager means negotiating with everyone from the people who rent props to representatives of a town where the production team might want to film on location.

Making arrangements is a big part of a production manager's job, so he or she will regularly come into contact with actors' agents, airline and hotel staffs, and transportation representatives (limousine drivers and truckers, etc.). Since they are in charge of the production budget, they also must work with accountants.

While they mostly perform their tasks in offices or at television studios, production managers also may work outdoors when they are on location. The hours that they work vary and may include time during evenings and weekends.

### Experience
The best experience for a job as a production manager—as it is for many jobs in television—is working in any capacity at a television station. Gaining experience through work as a production assistant is particularly helpful.

While you are in school, and even afterward, you can try working as a stage manager for a drama or theater group. These individuals perform a lot of the same tasks in the theater as production managers do at a television station. Experience as a business manager of some sort, even if it is outside the television industry, is also useful.

### Education and Training
Right now there are no education requirements to become a production manager. However, a college degree is useful. There are some classes you can concentrate on to better your chances of getting a job in this field. Business management, accounting, and general administrative courses are good, as are drama, art, and broadcast journalism classes.

## Salary

There is a wide range of salaries for production managers. According to one source, the pay typically averages out to be between $900 and $1,300 per week.

## SALES AND PROMOTIONS STAFF

Commercial television depends on advertising dollars to keep running. That is why sales and promotions staffs are an integral part of television production. Whether they work for a network selling high-priced ads during the Super Bowl or a tiny station in a small town selling thirty-second spots during the nightly newscast—or thinking up ways to get viewers to tune in—these individuals are vital to a station or network.

The most senior position on the promotions staff is the promotions manager. He or she has the job of supervising a staff of promotions specialists, overseeing the entire promotions program for the station, and organizing those programs. His or her goal is to give as much exposure to the station as possible while remaining within an allotted budget. Station promotions may include creating incentives for advertisers to buy airtime and gimmicks to make viewers watch certain programs. For example, the station may ask viewers to send in, on a postcard, the answer to a question that will be revealed during a particular time slot on a particular night, hoping to get them to tune in to the station at that time.

A community relations director oversees the programs and services that affect the community, such as personal appearances by television celebrities at their stations. They also hold forums, or meetings, with viewers in their area to listen to their concerns or to get input on how the station can better serve its audience.

Sales managers are in charge of sales representatives, whose job it is to get advertisers to buy airtime on their station. Sales managers assign each representative to a territory or to certain types of companies or businesses within a particular territory. They then must make sure that their team is performing well and settle any grievances the sales representatives may have. They also may service some of the bigger accounts themselves.

Sales representatives, or account executives, visit clients and try to get them to buy spots, or airtime, in which to run their company's commercials. These professionals need to be friendly, aggressive, and persistent. They work with clients, local business leaders, and even advertising agencies if the client has hired someone else to produce the commercials.

The creative services department of a television station does research to see which kinds of advertising and promotions would be most effective. It may help create the actual commercials.

## What to Expect

Key to being a sales representative or promotions staffer is the ability to sell. You have to believe in the product you are pushing, which is the value of airtime on your station, and get other people to believe in it, too. This means you should be creative, likable, a good talker, extroverted, and very motivated. That last item should not be difficult to come by. Since sales representatives are generally paid a commission, which is a percentage of a sale, they are motivated to make as many sales as possible.

As a sales or promotions worker, you will be asked to travel within your territory. However, you might also get to attend meetings and conferences in out-of-state locations.

While they do have deadlines, salespeople are more interested in quotas, which are the targeted numbers of sales that are set for each representative in a certain period of time. Under pressure to meet deadlines and quotas, these professionals may need to work long hours, sometimes even in the evenings or on weekends.

### Experience

In this field, any kind of sales experience is helpful, even working on the sales floor at a local clothing store. Of course, the closer you get to the kind of sales you will be doing as a television sales rep—maybe selling ad space for a newspaper, newsletter, or magazine—the better prepared you will be. Also, working your way up to some kind of managerial position shows that you have drive and ambition, and that you could take on the responsibility of being a sales manager.

### Education and Training

A bachelor's or master's degree in business administration is preferred by some employers, but usually a broad liberal arts education is enough to enter this field. Sales and promotions workers should definitely concentrate on classes in business, advertising, marketing, and public relations. Psychology, which can be used to help persuade clients and viewers, is a good choice, too, as are math, accounting, and economics. Some television production and computer science courses can help make you a more appealing candidate for this type of job. As always, gaining experience through an internship is highly recommended.

If you decide not to attend college, you can still further your education in ways that will help you break into this field. Many marketing and similar associations offer certificate programs in the sales and promotions field. For instance, Sales and Marketing Executives International offers a certificate in sales management. The criteria for granting the certificate is based both on classroom work and real-work performance. These programs typically offer courses in product management, sales management, promotions, and market research.

## Salary

The median yearly salary for sales managers is around $57,000, but keep in mind that that's an average. A lot depends on market size and how much their reps sell. Salaries in the smaller markets can be in the middle to high twenties, while sales managers in the largest markets can pull in more than $100,000.

Sales representatives can expect to earn $25,000 to $32,000 to start. These figures do not necessarily include bonuses for reaching sales goals or commissions.

**5**

# Behind the Scenes: Technical

If you are mechanically inclined, there is a place in television for you. Stations are always looking for people who can master the equipment that controls the lighting, picture, and sound of a broadcast.

## Broadcast Engineers

The technical professionals of television go by many different titles. They can be called operators, engineers, or technicians. These are the people who make sure that the mechanical part of a television broadcast goes off without a hitch.

There are a number of specific jobs that fall under the main heading of broadcast engineers. We are going to look at the primary occupations that fall under this category.

Chief engineers, transmission engineers, and broadcast field supervisors are the people who oversee, or are in charge of, the technicians who operate and maintain broadcasting equipment.

The cooperation of a number of engineers working together in a station's control room is necessary for a successful broadcast. These studio engineers operate a range of equipment within a studio, including cameras, the audio console, lighting, and other machines. At some stations, studio engineers may also deal with specialized equipment such as a character generator, which creates information—such as emergency weather warnings or subtitles for the hearing impaired—and scrolls it across a television screen.

Master control/videotape engineers are responsible for the parts of a show that are prerecorded. They operate the videotape recording and playback units that, for example, allow taped interviews and news stories to be run after the anchor introduces them during the live news broadcast. They are also the people who make sure commercials get run at the scheduled time.

What you see and hear is the work of light and sound engineers.

Video control engineers regulate how bright and clear a television picture is. Lighting technicians, also called electricians, control how the set or scene looks by adjusting the lights in the studio. They are also responsible for setting up and operating the lights.

Grips are people who often work closely with the electricians. They work with equipment related to lighting that does not have cords attached and deal with a lot of the rigging on a set, such as tracks and towers to support or move cameras and lights. They set up, maintain, and tear down the gear that removes, reflects, or otherwise manipulates the light.

Lighting technicians are overseen by a gaffer, who decides how much light is called for and what position the lights should be in, as well as how to blend colors and types of light, such as natural and fluorescent, to get the most natural, flattering, or revealing picture. In television dramas and sitcoms, as well as in commercials, where scenes may be shot out of order throughout any given day, gaffers need to keep track of lighting continuity. For example, they need to remember what time of day a particular scene is supposed to be taking place and arrange the lighting appropriately.

The person who holds the position one level below the gaffer is the best boy. The best boy is the gaffer's assistant. The term comes from the old days in Hollywood, in which someone would hire a gaffer to work on a movie and tell him to bring his "best boy" to help.

Sound quality and volume are controlled by audio control engineers. They work with boom operators, who handle microphones attached to long poles designed to get the mike close to whoever is speaking without it being seen on camera. Recording engineers oversee the operation and maintenance of video and sound recording equipment, as well as the machinery that produces special sound and visual effects.

Sound mixers perform their jobs after the fact. They take the videotaped or filmed version of a show and tinker with the sound quality. They also insert sounds and rerecord the voices of those on camera. This is called dubbing.

Location shoots are the domain of field technicians, who are in charge of all equipment that is used outside the studio. They work with transmitter operators, whose job is just what it sounds like; they operate transmitters. Their job is to check the signals from field equipment to make sure that the studio is receiving the broadcast transmission properly.

Finally, maintenance engineers make sure that electronic broadcast equipment is in working order and fix it when it malfunctions. They also are in charge of installing new or repaired equipment.

Broadcast and sound engineers, particularly studio engineers, need to be on the ball at all times during a broadcast. Part of their job involves juggling input from a number of different sources. They may be working with multiple cameras in the studio, or they may have to cut to a live broadcast and then work in a taped segment. They have to do it all on cue, at very specific times.

Broadcast technicians have to be good at working with their hands. They also have to be good at math and science to understand how the machinery they use works and how to get the most out of it. With all the new electronic equipment and the refinements made to the machines they already operate, broadcast and sound technicians need to keep up with current technology.

### What to Expect

In general, broadcast and sound technicians work indoors, in the control rooms of news stations and affiliates, or inside studios in Hollywood and other locations where entertainment television is produced. Yet there are times when they are required to travel and work on location, sometimes out-of-doors where the equipment is susceptible to the elements.

As with so many other positions in television, exactly what a broadcast or sound engineer does is dictated by where he or she works. Those who work for small stations in smaller markets are usually prone to the same catch-all type of work environment as their colleagues. Because the staffs of these stations may not be very large, everyone performs a variety of technical duties instead of sticking to just one. Technicians in larger markets and those who work directly for the networks get more of an opportunity to specialize.

Like their coworkers both on and off camera, broadcast and sound engineers work on deadline. The pressure can be intense, particularly for live broadcasts. The people who work in these positions work a forty-hour workweek, although overtime is not uncommon. Because so many television stations these days run continuously, or almost continuously, the hours that the staff is required to work are not strictly nine to five. In fact, those starting out in the field may have to take a job on the graveyard shift—late at night to early morning—and may have to work holidays and weekends.

Broadcast and sound technicians also need to take orders from directors and to think fast if a glitch occurs that interrupts transmission of a program. If a technician cannot fix a problem or fill airtime with something quickly, the result is dead air, or time in which nothing is being transmitted to the viewer.

Virtually any city large enough to have a television station needs to hire technicians, although the number and specific types of technician varies according to the equipment the station owns.

### Experience

Hands-on experience is, of course, the best way for a television engineer to get his or her training. Volunteering to work at a local station is a good move, as is apprenticing under an experienced engineer, which is similar to an internship. Apprentices are considered junior members of a staff who are there to learn a craft. Tinkering with electrical sound and lighting equipment on your own or as a member of a club at school can prepare you for the field as well.

Experience is crucial if you want to move to a larger market or a network position. These markets rarely take a chance on a newcomer, no matter how much training he or she may have.

Television engineers work their way up at smaller stations, learning as they go. The more successful they are at their duties, and the more they learn, the more valuable they become. They gradually take on more responsibilities and earn a reputation for knowing and performing their jobs well.

The outlook for employment in this field is reasonably good. New stations keep springing up, and many existing stations are expanding both their coverage and operating hours. Also, the technology used in broadcast television changes very quickly, which means that there is a demand for technicians to run the new equipment.

Whether it is because they think the hours and pay will be better somewhere else, or that there will be less pressure, many technicians end up leaving television to work in related jobs, such as with computers or as a Webmaster at a dot-com company. Several even strike out on their own and, using their knowledge of the current technology, start their own firms. All this is good news for those looking to become television technicians because for every person who leaves the field, there is one new opening.

### Education and Training

Training for a career as a broadcast or sound engineer can begin as early as junior high or high school. Those who want to succeed in this field need to concentrate on math and science classes. Becoming an amateur or "ham" radio operator, or even owning a police scanner or some kind of CB equipment, can teach you a lot about electronics and the transmission of sound waves.

Working at a local cable access station or, if there is one, your high school or college television station is a great learning experience. Actually doing the work you would do as a technician, applying the things you may have learned in the classroom, teaches you the lessons you need to learn.

Even if your school doesn't have a television station, chances are it does have some kind of radio program. Even if it is just a brief news and announcements program broadcast from the principal's office, you will be gaining valuable experience. The sound equipment used in these instances is often similar to, if not the same as, that used for television. Learning how to operate this equipment is what's important. Those who want to concentrate on lights and visuals also can get practical training working on the stage crew of their school's drama department.

There are school programs and degrees that focus on technical learning to be found at most liberal arts colleges and universities. Some of the better programs are found at schools with good reputations for film or journalism studies, such as Columbia University and UCLA.

Most broadcast technicians earn at least an associate's degree. If you want to be promoted to chief engineer, you will more than likely need a four-year college degree. This is especially the case if you work at a large station or for one of the major networks.

Trade schools are another way to learn to become a television engineer. Trade or technical-school programs concentrate on only one field of work, or trade. Usually, these programs teach you all the same technical knowledge you would learn in a college or university program, only it is much more concentrated. You will not get a diploma from a trade school, but if you pass the courses they teach, you will get a certificate that states that you understand and are capable of performing the tasks you studied.

The nice thing about trade schools is that the people on staff often will help you find a job after you finish their program, or they may help set you up with an apprenticeship under an experienced professional.

While the FCC no longer requires that broadcast technicians be licensed, certification is like a seal of approval that tells prospective employers that you are competent and knowledgeable. In addition to trade schools, associations such as the Society of Broadcast Engineers offer certification to those who know their craft and can pass a written exam.

Just because you've landed a job doesn't mean the learning stops. Technology changes all the time, and successful broadcast technicians need to keep up with the latest developments. There are refresher courses available in most communities.

## Salary

As with other jobs in television, the higher salaries are found in the big cities and markets. Also, jobs in commercial television pay more than those with public broadcast stations. Because it is not supported by commercial income, public broadcasting funnels a higher percentage of its money into programming than it does into salaries.

The yearly income for broadcast and sound technicians averages around $25,000. The range starts in the high teens and tops off at around $67,000.

Freelance sound and light technicians get paid on a per-diem basis, which means they get paid by the day. Depending on their experience, they make $300 to $400 dollars for a ten- to twelve-hour day. Keep in mind, however, that most freelance sound technicians have to either buy or rent their equipment, which is very expensive. This can take a big bite out of their salaries.

## CAMERA OPERATORS

You've heard it before: A picture is worth a thousand words. Since television is a visual medium, which means it relies heavily on pictures, you can imagine how important camera operators are to the business.

Television camera operators film or tape a wide range of subjects, including news reports, commercials, documentaries, and television series and movies. They work with writers and reporters to tell a story.

Camera operators need to have a good eye, which means they can spot the best scene to shoot and the best angle and lighting in which to shoot it. For instance, they may draw attention to a particular part of the scene they are shooting by focusing on certain objects and blurring the background.

Other qualities essential to being a successful television camera operator include good hand-eye coordination and artistic ability. Because they are on their feet almost all the time they are working, they also should be physically fit and should have good endurance—their days are often long and tiring. They should be patient, as they may have to wait to get the perfect shot or to film a busy or elusive interview subject, and they should pay close attention to detail, to make sure all the right elements appear in each frame of their work.

There is a lot of equipment associated with being a television camera operator. In addition to the cameras themselves, these professionals deal with different kinds of film and videotape, lenses, filters, tripods, and various sorts of lighting equipment.

Studio camera operators work in a broadcast studio and usually film their subjects from a fixed position using large stationary cameras. Those who operate cameras for news operations are known as electronic news gathering, or ENG, operators. In addition to operating the video camera and sound equipment on location, ENG crews must also know how to work complex transmission equipment to send, or feed, their footage back to the studio for broadcast. ENG operators should know how to edit because they may need to cut and splice tape on the run to put together a package for quick relay back to the station.

Television camera operators can also work with cameras placed on a track, so that the action can be shot in motion from different angles or directions. To accomplish this, the camera operator who is shooting the scene will be pushed or pulled along the track by grips. Stedicams track motion, too, but they do so attached to a harness that the operator wears, so that the picture is less jiggly or out of focus.

## What to Expect
Those in entry-level jobs usually start out learning how to set up lights, cameras, and other associated

equipment. The more experience you gain, the more responsibility you will be given.

Studio news camera operators usually know when they will be on the job—they work whenever the station airs its daily newscasts. Other television camera operators are not always so lucky. Their working hours are erratic, since they work around whatever the current production schedule demands.

Except for studio operators, there is no such thing as a set environment for camera operators. Working conditions can vary quite a bit. You may work in a studio, or you may find yourself in the middle of a busy street. For example, news camera operators are often required to be outside and may have to deal with dangerous or unpleasant surroundings. They might need to be on location late at night or in the middle of a snowstorm or hurricane.

Mostly, though, there are more ordinary dangers associated with being a television camera operator. There is the physical strain of hauling heavy equipment and the mental or emotional strain of being stressed out about deadlines.

The good news is that every television station—from independent and cable stations to networks and their affiliates—employs camera operators. No matter how small the market, there needs to be at least one video camera operator for there to be a television broadcast.

The bad news is that there are many people who want these jobs, so the competition for them is pretty tough. A way around that is to try to get work on a freelance basis, which might be possible in news operations in smaller markets. However, as with all freelancers, independent television camera operators usually spend most of their time trying to line up jobs and get paid for work they have already done.

Those who have the most skills and talent are the ones who will land good jobs in this field and keep them. Having a specialty, such as a background in computers or electronics, can help set you apart from the crowd and get you a job.

Camera operators work most closely with directors, actors, and camera assistants.

### Experience

The best way to learn how to be a television camera operator is to get your hands on some equipment and use it. This can be as simple as using a plain old 35 mm camera and taking still shots, or borrowing your family's video camera to record a birthday party. You may also want to get involved in your university's community television station, which should give you access to some of the more complicated, expensive machinery.

Another way to get experience is to take classes in broadcast journalism or movie and television production. While in these programs, you will be required to produce work that will be judged and graded. More important, you will be able to get your hands on professional equipment and gain experience with it. As always, internships and apprenticeships are excellent ways to gain experience.

### Education and Training

Although talent and being able to use a camera are the most important factors for a career in camera work, a college degree may be required for you to get hired as a television camera operator. Many universities and colleges have programs in photography or film, as do vocational and trade schools.

The programs in all of these places usually cover the basics, such as equipment and film processing, as well as special techniques used by professional camera operators. Art classes are also helpful in that they help develop an eye for composition.

Community education classes in the use of a camera do not offer a degree or certificate, but they can give you an introduction to photography. You could take one of these classes to see if you really like the field.

There are several ways outside the classroom to learn how to operate a camera. You can join a photography or camera club at school, or try to get a job at a photography studio or store. Reading photography magazines will help keep you abreast of the latest technology in cameras. It's also a great way to learn about the trade.

A lot of the newer equipment involves some type of computer technology, so learning about computers and computer editing software can be an important part of preparing for a job as a camera operator.

## Salary
The salary range for those working in the news end of this field runs anywhere between $15,000 to $30,000, depending on one's skill level and experience. Some of the most highly paid camera operators in news are paid $44,000 or more. The larger the market you are in, and the higher the cost of living in the area where you work, the more money you can expect to make.

Those working on entertainment shows are usually paid more. Camera operators who are busy make in the realm of $70,000 to $80,000 per year.

Union camera operators make $50 per hour. They also get a twelve-hour guarantee, which means that they get paid for twelve hours of work even if they are not on the job for twelve hours. This twelve-hour pay includes four hours of overtime at time and a half ($75 per hour). If they work for more than twelve hours, they are on "gold time" and get paid double, or $100 per hour.

# 6

# Creative Support

When we think of the creative side of television, most of us immediately think of actors, writers, and directors. Yet there are several creative individuals employed in television whose work we may take for granted. What these jobs are and the duties they involve is the subject of this chapter.

## DESIGNERS

Designers are people who figure out how something should look and figure out the best way to create this vision. They have to mix form with function. In television production, there are set, lighting, and costume designers who create the sets, lighting schemes, and clothing used in the production of a television show.

Designers need to be creative and imaginative. They have to have a good eye for color, shapes, angles, and size, and be able to pay attention to detail.

Good communication skills are essential to being a designer. These professionals must clearly convey to clients the images in their head and do so using verbal, written, and visual means of communication.

Designers create sketches to see how an idea might actually look. These are pen-and-paper or computer-drawn versions of how a costume or set is supposed to look. Therefore, the ability to draw is key to success as a designer.

To do their jobs well, designers need to read a program's script, or perhaps even talk with the screenwriter, to get a feel for things such as what time period the story takes place in, what the characters are like, and what action is taking place in certain parts of the story. They also need to speak with the director and others involved with the production to make sure their designs not only look good but will perform as needed.

For instance, a costume designer might create an elaborate dress with all sorts of buttons and hooks, but if the character wearing it has to change clothes quickly, the designer has to make sure the dress is easy to get out of. Likewise, parts of a set might look good on camera, but perhaps that cool coffee table is too big and the actors keep bumping into it. Set designers have to make sure that those on camera can move freely around a set.

Designers must be good at budgeting. They need to budget both a studio's or network's money and their own time. Because designers are often working on their own, they should be self-motivated enough to accomplish the job without someone watching over them constantly.

### What to Expect
Designers work according to the schedule of the person or company that hires them. For instance, they may need to meet with the director during normal business hours or later in the evening, depending on when the director is free. In addition, they will often leave a meeting and then continue working, drawing sketches and putting the finishing touches on a design, or investigating the price of fabric or other materials they need.

Designers can work long hours, which get even longer as their deadlines loom and the production is ready to start filming.

While they are somewhat independent and have a certain amount of freedom, designers also need to work as part of a production team. They frequently must consult with directors, producers, camera operators, and even actors.

Having this many people involved in the process increases the chance that someone along the line is not going to like a certain design. Designers cannot only please themselves or get lost in the beauty of their creations. They have to be able to face rejection and have to start all over again, perhaps altering their art to please somebody higher up the chain of command.

As a set, lighting, or costume designer, you may have an assistant or two working with you, depending on the size of the market and the production's budget.

There is a lot of competition for work as a designer, just as with so many other jobs in television. Your chances for landing a job are much better if you have formal education in the field, as well as experience and well-developed talent.

### Experience

Designers get experience by creating. Those who want to become set and lighting designers should volunteer to work on a school or community theater production. Costume designers can get experience simply by fashioning and sewing their own outfits or clothes.

Once you have a few designs that you think are good, the next step is to put together a portfolio. This is a collection of examples of your work. A design portfolio can include sketches and/or pictures of finished sets or costumes.

## Education and Training

Set, lighting, and costume designers typically have at least a bachelor's degree, if not a master of fine arts degree (MFA). Many colleges and universities offer programs that allow you to get a degree in one of these fields.

There are also schools that specialize in design, such as the Pratt School of Design in New York City, which focuses on clothing. Students who want to attend these schools must not only have good grades and academic skills, but they must prove they have artistic talent as well. To apply to these schools you must have a portfolio of your work. If you are unsure about how to create a presentable portfolio, your high school art teacher may be able to help you.

In addition to classes in art history, design, textiles, and architecture, it is helpful if prospective designers take courses in business and marketing. Some designers work on a freelance basis, and they need to know how to sell themselves and their services.

Knowing how to use a computer is helpful, too. In place of a flat drawing, designers may be able to create a three-dimensional model of a television set or costume. Computer-aided design speeds things up by allowing the designer to make changes with a few keystrokes. Computers also allow designers more flexibility in where they do their work. Because electronic "sketches" can be e-mailed within seconds, a designer in one city can work with a production based in another location.

## Salary
The latest reports on salaries for designers state that the average annual income is about $30,000. Of course, beginners make quite a bit less, around $19,000 a year. The pros who have been at this a while can earn closer to $70,000 or more.

## WARDROBE PEOPLE/COSTUMERS
Wardrobe people make, take care of, shop for, and keep track of the costumes. They are also responsible for accessories such as jewelry, hats, and purses. They research, find, buy, clean, repair, and otherwise maintain the costumes and accessories that will be used during a television shoot. Sometimes they also help get actors into and out of difficult costumes such as suits of armor or other period clothing.

Those in charge of wardrobe must make sure that the costumes and clothing necessary for a day's shoot are on the set and in good condition. To accomplish this task, they may be required to clean, iron, or sew, sometimes at a moment's notice.

Wardrobe people need to have good tailoring skills and be able to mend or dye different types of fabric. They also need to have a sense of fashion.

While they do work on their own quite a bit, wardrobe people are part of the production team. They need good communication skills and they must know how to take orders because they work with production staff, actors, and costume designers.

Knowledge of television production is important, too. Wardrobe people should be able to read a script and anticipate what costumes will be needed from one scene to the next. A working knowledge of things like lighting, so that they can understand how certain costumes or alterations they make are going to look on camera, is a plus.

## What to Expect
Wardrobe people may be required to work indoors or outdoors, depending on where the scenes of a program are being filmed or taped. When on location, most wardrobe people work out of the back of a truck that houses all of the costumes and accessories they will need that day.

Working long hours is pretty common. Wardrobe people need to be on the set the whole time the production is shooting, and they also need to be around both before the shoot and afterward, gathering up all the costumes used and preparing for the next day.

## Experience
Work done either in the clothing industry or backstage in a theater offers good experience for this type of occupation. Any kind of sewing or tailoring experience, like designing your own patterns and making the garments, is good, too.

## Education and Training
The education level of wardrobe people can vary. Those who work in wardrobe pick up many skills while actually performing their tasks. Some of these professionals have a college degree, but it is not required. Certainly a degree in fashion design from a university or design school can be very helpful, especially if you choose one located in an area where a lot of filming takes place, like New York City or Los Angeles.

## Salary

Those starting out as wardrobers generally earn annual salaries in the high teens. Those who have been at this a while and have earned a solid reputation, as well as those who work on projects with large budgets, can earn a few thousand dollars a week.

## HAIRSTYLISTS AND MAKEUP ARTISTS

These professionals create the hair and makeup styles for those who appear on camera. Some specialize in special effects, using makeup and prosthetic devices to create creatures, make actors look older, or devise realistic-looking wounds. Others work to make sure that the actors look good or that their looks are appropriate for the characters they are playing.

Hairstylists working for a television show perform many of the same duties that any hairdresser does. They wash, cut, and style hair. They also work with wigs and other artificial hairpieces.

How a makeup artist applies makeup for television requires special skills. What may look good in person might be too washed out on the television screen. Likewise, you don't want an actor to appear as if he or she is plastered with makeup. A makeup person has to apply special stage makeup in just the right amounts.

Hairstylists and makeup artists are also responsible for providing all of their own tools and makeup. They must keep their tools and work areas clean and germ-free.

Those who work with hair and makeup need to be creative and have a sense of style. They must not only know about current products, looks, and styles here in America, but also the styles of many different cultures and eras. The look they create for an actor has to make sense in the context of the story that is being told, including where and when it is taking place and the personality of the character that is being portrayed. Those who work in fantasy, science fiction, or special effects need to have vivid imaginations and must not be afraid to experiment.

In addition, hairstylists and makeup professionals must have a working knowledge of all phases of television production, especially of camera operation and lighting. These two items can alter appearance and affect how an actor or anchor looks. For instance, a certain camera angle may not be flattering to an actor, maybe drawing attention to a crooked nose or broad chin. Knowing this, a makeup artist could apply cosmetics in such a way that the flaw is reduced on camera. Likewise, hair and makeup people must be aware of what the heat and stress of lights can do to their work, so they can be ready for touch-ups as needed.

If you're working on someone's hair or face, you're going to get up close and personal with that person. That's why a hair or makeup artist needs to be a "people person" with good communication skills. He or she also needs to not tire easily, because these jobs require a lot of standing.

## What to Expect

Hairstylists and makeup people are usually employed by a studio, station, or network. However, there are freelance hair and makeup artists who get paid by the day or week. Sometimes actors or anchors will like the work of one particular person and hire him or her to do their hair and makeup for every project—sometimes even for personal appearances such as premieres and awards shows.

Television hair and makeup people generally work in a space somewhere behind the scenes of a studio or station. On location, they usually work out of a trailer that is set up like a mobile beauty salon.

Beginners may very likely start out as assistants or apprentices. In addition to relatively easy tasks with regard to hair and makeup styling, they may be expected to run errands or research and purchase products.

### Education and Training

Hair and makeup artists are professionals who are licensed in hair care and styling, as well as makeup application. To earn the license, they must have some kind of training in cosmetology, which is the science of hairdressing and makeup application.

There are vocational schools that teach the art of hair and makeup styling. They teach skills such as hair cutting and coloring, scalp treatments, and makeup analysis and application. In addition, courses on hygiene, basic anatomy, and chemistry are provided, as are business and communications classes.

Those enrolled in one of these vocational schools can expect to devote one to two years, on average, to studying. Apprenticing with a professional, which is much like interning, can add another year or two to the training.

Once they have graduated from a vocational training program, students are ready to take the licensing examination, which typically involves passing a written exam and performing hairstyling and makeup application to the satisfaction of an examiner. Some states make students describe verbally what they are doing and why when they take the hands-on part of the test.

You do not need any other academic degree in order to attend beauty school. There are a few places that, as long as the person is at least sixteen years old, require hair and makeup artists to have only a junior high school education. The majority, however, prefer candidates to have at least a high school diploma.

The requirements for licensing vary from state to state, and a license to operate in one state may not be valid in another. Hair and makeup artists must be sure they can legally operate in the state where they live and work.

Learning continues even after a hair or makeup artist is licensed and finds work. Styles change, as do hair products and cosmetics. Hairstylists and makeup artists need to attend seminars and workshops to keep up with trends and new products.

## Salary

In television, there are makeup department heads and  key makeup and hair people, who work regularly for a certain star or show. There are also department artists, who may be hired by a production company to work on whoever needs attention, usually people besides the star or stars of a show or television movie. Then there are day artists. They are hired on an on-call basis, whenever there is too much work for the key or department artists to handle.

Makeup department heads earn the most money, usually about $35 per hour. The usual rate for a key makeup artist, who works under the department head, is a little less. They typically earn about $33 per hour. Day artists earn about the same as key artists. Those starting out, or who work as assistants, make less.

## VISUAL ARTISTS

When you think about the different jobs in television, you probably don't consider illustrators and graphic artists. That's because you are probably more used to seeing their work on printed pages or the Internet. But visual artists do have a place in a television studio. They are generally background players whose work adds to the overall atmosphere of a set.

Imagine if you were watching the news and all you saw behind the anchors was a blank white wall. That would be pretty boring, right? Illustrators and graphic artists help fix situations like that. They use their talent to draw and paint the set to enhance what you see on television.

Their job is to create backgrounds that give the illusion that you're viewing someplace other than a studio. Sometimes their work just dresses up a set. To do this, they use a variety of different materials, including oil and watercolor paints, pencils, chalk, and computers.

There are several different types of visual artists who work in television. Illustrators are often used to draw storyboards for television programs and commercials. Storyboards present action in a series of pictures that give executives a clear idea about content, and map out where actors should stand and where cameras should be placed. Animators are the people who bring cartoons to life. They draw and color frames, known as cels, and then run them all together to make them move. In television, the most typical job for graphic designers is to create the opening and closing credits for programs.

Virtual set designers create backdrops for television entertainment and news shows. Using computers, they can turn a studio or set into an outdoor playground or a busy city street.

Art directors are the people who oversee the work of other visual artists. They figure out the overall look of a set or scene and check to make sure the finished product lives up to expectations.

The prerequisites for becoming a visual artist are being able to draw or paint and to communicate well, both in words and in pictures.

## What to Expect

Visual artists work in art studios, which are a well-lit, comfortable places where they can be creative. Some studios may have a drafting table, which is a specially designed desk that is set at an angle.

Visual artists work their way up the ladder by creating good work and by meeting deadlines. Like many artists who paint portraits and still-life pictures, illustrators and graphic artists may very well create their own signature style.

Developing a relationship with a major studio or design firm is a great way to find steady work. Those hired by these employers usually work normal hours. However, rush jobs are not out of the question, so overtime may be required.

Many graphic designers and illustrators do fairly well working freelance. The only catch is that the work may not be as steady, and they spend a lot of time drumming up business and sending out invoices to get paid.

The need for visual artists in all fields, including television, continues to grow. Animation is a particularly popular field, as animated series keep dominating

Saturday morning shows and prime-time animated series continue to be in demand.

### Experience

Perhaps the best way for a visual artist to gain experience is to enroll in a design program through a university or community education program.

While in college, an internship will add to your marketability. Working in an art studio or for a design firm not only offers a chance to create work, but also lets you see other visual artists in action.

As with designers, visual artists should have a solid portfolio of their work ready to show prospective employers.

### Education and Training

There is no set level of education required to become a visual artist. Generally, illustrators and graphic artists have at least a bachelor's degree. The main subjects for a degree in one of these fields include art, art history, and computer graphics.

However, developing your artistic talent is crucial for this job. Whether it is in a degree program or at the side of a professional artist, hands-on training is the best way for a visual artist to succeed.

### Salary

The average salary for a visual artist employed by a design studio runs in the low thirties. The lowest paid earn around $18,000, while those in the highest brackets usually make around $65,000. Freelance salaries vary, since beginners don't charge as much as someone with more experience and credentials.

## STUNT PLAYERS

Stunt players use special equipment, acrobatic abilities, and a sense of fearlessness to perform activities that may be too dangerous or specialized for an actor. These stunts include anything from taking a punch to "flying" by a wire harness to dangling from the ledge of a tall building.

A stunt player's job can be a dangerous one, but a large part of that job is making sure the danger is minimal. Safety is a big concern for those who perform stunts. They spend a lot of time preparing, choreographing every move beforehand, rehearsing their stunts, and making sure all appropriate safeguards are in place.

Believe it or not, stunt players need to be decent actors, too. It's not enough just to fall several stories or take a punch. They need to fill in for the actor and make the scene look realistic. Like the actors they are subbing for, they need to understand a character's motivation and what a scene's setup is so they can make the audience believe what is happening on-screen.

These professionals need to know the proper use of the specialized equipment of their trade, items such as a harness for flying, minitrampolines, and airbags. Because of the hazardous nature of their jobs, stunt players should also have a basic knowledge of first aid.

Good flexibility, coordination and overall physical fitness are three main traits of a successful stunt player. Mental fitness is also a key component. Stunt players need to have nerves of steel, to be sure of themselves, and to be confident of their abilities. If they go into a dangerous stunt halfheartedly, or without thinking everything through beforehand, they increase the chances that something may go wrong and they will be injured.

## What to Expect

Stunt players are hired based on their previous work, including what stunts they specialize in, as well as physical resemblance to the actor for whom they will be subbing. Stuntpeople generally work on a short-term basis, and employment can be very spotty.

Stunt players with several years of experience can work their way into the position of stunt coordinator. Working with directors, screenwriters, producers, crew, and actors, stunt coordinators have plenty of input into what stunts can be done and how they should be executed. Stunt coordinators study the script, review what the director wants, and know what equipment will be needed, where to get it, and where to find the stuntpeople who can perform the necessary stunts.

## Education and Training

There are no specific educational requirements for stuntpeople. They receive most of their training on the job. However, studying drama, physical education, and first aid are all useful in this career.

## Experience

There is no specific job or hobby designed to prepare you for a career as a stunt player. The best experience is doing the kinds of things stunt performers do as part of their job. Taking classes in expert driving, the martial arts, or gymnastics can keep a prospective stunt player limber and ready to perform when he or she lands work. Some of the best preparation for entering this field is participating in sports. Having participated as an actor in an amateur theater, film, or television production is good experience to have as well.

## Salary

How much a stunt player gets paid depends on how much work he or she does, as well as the type of stunt and how dangerous it is. Some of these men and women earn between $400 and $600 a day.

## AGENTS AND PUBLICISTS

The primary goal of agents and publicists is to make their clients successful. Agents hustle to line up jobs for their clients. They work with on-screen talent, but they also have screenwriters and other members of the behind-the-scenes crew as clients. Agents are employed by talent agencies, the biggest and best known of which operate out of New York City and Los Angeles.

Agents advise their clients on the best way to run their careers, from what specific jobs to take to how much money they should get paid. They get their clients interviews or auditions, and negotiate contracts.

Agents deal with directors, casting agents, producers, and attorneys on a regular basis. They also frequently work with publicists, who arrange for photo shoots, press conferences, and public appearances. They issue press releases to keep the media up-to-date on any news regarding their clients.

Like agents, publicists are employed to make their clients look good. They are in charge of getting media attention for their clients. They make sure a client's name is recognized by the people who do the hiring.

Agents and publicists must know how both the television and media businesses work. They need to have good communication skills, both verbal and written, and they must be willing to work under pressure. They also must be aggressive and persistent.

## What to Expect

Agents spend a lot of time on the phone and in meetings, talking up their clients and discussing projects. Beginners also have to deal with low wages and long hours spent entertaining and reassuring their clients. Many times new agents and publicists are paired up with fresh, unknown talent as their clients.

Turnover for agents is high, especially during the first few years. It has been estimated that some 30 percent quit the field because the stress is too much, or the duties, at first, are dull, or the paycheck is too small.

Those who stick it out, though, may be rewarded. Sometimes, after as few as five years, a person can rise to become a senior agent. Contact with stars and high-level entertainment executives becomes more frequent and fulfilling. The hours are still long, but the pay is better.

## Experience

Agents and publicists can gain experience by interning with an agency while in college. Joining groups such as the Association of Talent Agents and the Public Relations Society of America will give you details about work as an agent or publicist, and will allow you to do some intense networking.

The most important thing you can do to get experience as an agent or publicist is to practice. This could mean something as simple as volunteering to write a newsletter or mingling at parties. You want to get experience communicating with people in written and spoken forms because that is a large part of what people in these professions do.

## Education

Most talent agencies prefer hiring people who have a bachelor's degree. They suggest taking courses in marketing, advertising, communications, creative writing, statistical analysis, and business.

To eventually move into a senior agent or management position, it doesn't hurt to have an advanced degree in public relations, public affairs, political science, or business administration.

Some associations, such as the Public Relations Society of America, also offer certification programs. This type of certification is simply an extra weapon you might wish to have in the employment wars. To get certified, you must have a certain number of years worth of experience in public relations and pass a written test.

## Salary

As mentioned before, starting salaries for agents are low, usually around $16,000. After a couple of years, it rises to the middle twenties or so, and then can travel up into the low forties.

These figures take into account base pay only. Agents typically earn a percentage of what their clients earn, too. The more a client makes, the more the agent gets. Agents who represent big stars—who pull in big salaries—can make a great deal of money.

# 7

## Voices of Experience

You can take classes and learn the theory behind different jobs in television, but there is no substitute for experience. This chapter offers words of wisdom from television professionals in a number of positions.

### MEET A SCREENWRITER

Larry Brody is an accomplished screenwriter and producer who lives in Los Angeles. He has written hundreds of hours of network television programs, including episodes of *Diagnosis Murder, Star Trek: Voyager, Star Trek: The Next Generation*, and *Walker, Texas Ranger*. He also has created and produced several animated series and written a number of network movies of the week.

Brody managed, with the help of a relative, to obtain an agent while he was a student at Northwestern University. After finishing graduate school, he moved to Hollywood.

His big break as a screenwriter came when an actor looking to make a comeback convinced Brody to write a script for a proposed television series. The plan was that the actor would try to sell, or pitch, the series to a number of producers he knew, and when it actually got on the air, he would star in it. All he needed was the right script, and he wanted Brody to write it.

One executive who received the script liked the writing and wanted Brody's agent to send more of the writer's work his way. Although neither the series nor the television movie script that the agent sent got produced, Brody had at least made it into the loop. The fact that he had written a script that an executive had asked for, or commissioned, was enough to open doors to more work.

Brody has this to say to those trying to break into the screenwriting business:

> *To prepare for a career as a writer you have to, first of all, write. That means being on the school newspaper, Web site, literary magazine, or whatever. It also means writing for your own enjoyment.*
>
> *If you're involved in a drama group, in or out of school, see if you can write a play for it. Whether the play is good or bad doesn't matter. What matters is what you learned about writing by doing the writing. It's also important that you finish. Learning to finish what you start writing is one of the toughest and most important lessons.*
>
> *You also have to read as much as you can and (parents and teachers aren't going to like this) watch as much television and film as you can. That's because this is the best way to learn the storytelling patterns in different genres and have them become ingrained in your consciousness, so you can tell your own stories properly. You also learn the timing of the scenes, how long they are, etc. And you learn what subjects or ideas you would like to write about and what ones you wouldn't.*
>
> *A beginner should write some scripts on his or her own and then start shopping for an agent. The important*

*thing will be to get an agent who believes in the writer and pushes him or her, getting producers and executives to read the writer's scripts so they can see how good the writer is. Then they'll hire him or her. This sometimes happens fast, but it can also take a very long time.*

*The way you get a job in television is to write your sample script and get it to someone who likes it enough to let you pitch to his or her series. That means you can go in and try to convince the person to let you write one of your ideas. If you succeed, the person hires you to write it. If you come close, he or she asks you to come back with more ideas. If you fail, the person just says thanks.*

*After you've written some episodes this way (freelance), you may be asked to become a staff writer on a show that really likes your work. Now you come to work every day and hang out, but you get paid a weekly salary plus a fee for each script you write. From here, you work your way up to being the executive producer of your own show.*

*Knowing someone is always helpful. If I hadn't met that actor I might still be looking for a break. Networking is crucial. You have to become part of a local artistic community, whether it be at your school or outside of it. You have to know and become real friends with other writers and people in related creative fields. That way, as they move upward and into the "big time," they will want to help you, to take you with them. Also, if they know someone who can help, and you're a friend, then you'll get to meet that person, too, and maybe be helped yourself.*

*My friends and I all started out as unemployed wanna-bes. Some became writers, some actors, some network executives. But by staying friendly with each other we get to work together and keep each other employed. In fact, my big regret is that I didn't stay friendly with enough of my old buds.*

*The upside to the television writing business is that you get to express yourself to a huge audience and make a great deal of money. The downside is that unless you're very, very lucky or play way ahead like a chess player, your career is always iffy, with many ups and downs. Every time you finish a job it's like starting over again. You're always selling yourself.*

*My advice is to learn your art as well as you can. Write, write, and then write some more. Keep an open mind and know that you never know it all. Don't be intimidated. Come to L.A. and give it your best shot. Believe in yourself. Don't give up.*

*Oh, and find a great day job just on the offhand, impossible chance that you—sob—fail.*

## MEET A TELEVISION JOURNALIST

Though she now works for a newspaper, Lynette spent seven years as a television journalist, starting out at a station in Lubbock, Texas, while she earned her bachelor's degree in journalism.

She has held a number of jobs in the field. At first her experiences landed squarely on the production side, where she did everything from working the TelePrompTer (the machine that scrolls the text for anchors to read) to audio to running tapes. Later, after she graduated, Lynette became a director. Even though that position "was the top of the ladder on that kind of work," she says, she knew it wasn't the career for her. She wanted to get outside the studio and meet with people, find out what their concerns were, and let others know what was happening. She wanted to be a reporter.

Lynette talked the news director at her station into giving her a shot at the daily agriculture report. Growing up on a farm, she had always been around crops and animals. Armed with that and her degree in journalism, the position seemed like a natural fit.

"At first, I was basically the camerawoman for it, but with the idea, all along, that I'd eventually be a reporter for it," she says.

Not only was Lynette the reporter, she was also anchor for the agriculture report. She knew all along she would not just be able to sit behind a desk and read stories handed to her by others.

"Basically, when I was not delivering it as an anchor, I did all these other things," she says. "I found the stories, shot the stories, reported the stories, wrote the stories, edited the stories, and then delivered the stories as an anchor—all of these things under one umbrella."

Her workday was very rarely short, usually lasting eight hours or longer. Particularly because she produced a segment that ran early in the morning and at noon, she didn't have a normal nine-to-five schedule, either.

"I would get in there around 5:30 AM, and then I'd be off by the middle of the afternoon," she says.

"A typical day was getting up, and then, first thing in the morning, the Ag Update. After I got off the air, I'd basically just start looking through the wires, collecting stories, getting set up for the day. Then, many times, I would have something scheduled for maybe nine in the morning. So I'd go out and do that, shoot video, interview people for the story, then bring it back. Usually on my way back I'd start organizing my thoughts. Back at my desk, I would start writing that story and editing it.

"So that'd be a typical day, right there. I mean, that would take up my whole day."

Sometimes keeping up that schedule took its toll on Lynette.

"For me, I think that in the job that I had, there were probably a few too many responsibilities. Basically, I felt like sometimes I was doing a little bit too much to sit down and really enjoy any part of it. I just, many times, felt rushed, and I think sometimes that really takes out the fun part of it.

"I'm glad I did it when I did it. I don't know if I was still there today if I'd be able to do it because with that pace, it's just go, go, go. And if it isn't go, go, go, then you're not getting fresh information on the screen for your viewers at home."

Despite the long hours and the early wake-up calls, Lynette has good feelings about her time in television news.

"I really enjoyed finding out what made people tick," she says. "I really liked finding out the essence of their lives, their livelihoods. When I could get these farmers to really share with me and not have a barrier—not keep me at arm's distance but really open up—that was really rewarding."

She would recommend television journalism to anyone interested in the field.

"I think it's an open opportunity for anyone," Lynette says. "The important thing is, you have to let the person in charge know that you are interested in doing it and that you are capable. You have to be persistent."

## MEET AN ACTRESS

Kathryn Joosten didn't set out to be an actress. She originally went to school to study nursing and worked for ten years in Chicago as a psychiatric nurse. After she left that profession, she says, she "had a succession of survival jobs, eventually selling advertising."

Joosten started acting in community theater in the Chicago area. She says she really lucked out by landing the first television gig she ever auditioned for—playing a Lotto ball in a commercial.

Since then, Joosten has been able to make quite a decent living acting in films, theater, and television. Her television credits include guest-starring roles on series such as *N.Y.P.D. Blue, Seinfeld, Frasier,* and *E.R.* She says she is most proud of her recurring role as the president's secretary, Mrs. Landingham, on the NBC show *The West Wing.*

Joosten estimates her annual yearly income is in the $150,000 to $200,000 ballpark. She realizes that she's one of the lucky ones. "The majority of actors who belong to the Screen Actors Guild, one of our unions, make less than $10,000 a year," she says.

She admits that finding steady work as an actor is tough because the competition is so fierce. "There are just too many applicants for each position that opens. In television and film, there are just so many parts in a year, and ten times that number of actors who want to get one of those parts," she says.

The world of acting can be filled with many ups and downs. "When you achieve some success, it's the greatest.

However, when you're just struggling it can be terribly depressing," she says.

People who want to be actors should be ready to deal with rejection. But they must not take it personally, says Joosten.

"Most important is the ability to accept rejection as a part of the job picture, not as a rejection of oneself. Many actors, especially young ones, have so much of their own identities so closely woven into their acting that they cannot separate themselves from the business of acting. I've always felt that beginning actors should have some kind of real business experiences so that they can realize much of this career is business."

What can you do to prepare for a career in acting? Joosten suggests you join a theater group, either in your school or out in the community.

"Try to learn as much about the technical end of it as the acting end," she adds. "Know how to do lights, sound, sets. All of the skills you acquire will help you move up the ladder."

She would advise against banking everything on your eventual success as an actor. "There's a reason why so many actors are waiters," says Joosten. "They need to make a living while they look for work as an actor.

"Learn some kind of skill that will allow you to find a survival job—we call them McJobs—that will allow you the freedom to audition during the day and take occasional acting jobs," she advises. "Think about computing. There are great night jobs in that field, as well as self-employment."

So what does it take to make it as an actor? Talent, of course, but that's not all. "One has to have incredible endurance, and a large amount of just plain luck—

being the right person for the right part, at the right time, for the right producer," Joosten says.

"Here's the bottom line. For every part available in television there are at least 100 aspirants who want that part. It is a combination of connections, agency, talent, and luck that determines who gets the part. You may notice that I have not listed talent as the most important component. That's because there is a surplus of talent for every part available. It's the other factors that determine whether or not that talent gets a shot."

Then, perhaps harkening back to her first television job, Joosten says of acting, "Personally, I've always looked at it as my own personal lotto!

"At the bottom of all this, however, is that you must have the skills and talent to deliver when all the rest of it falls into place."

Would she recommend acting as a profession? Absolutely. "I love it," she says.

## MEET A NEWS DIRECTOR

Bill is the news director of a station in a middle market in upstate New York.

While television journalism can be glamorous, Bill always keeps in mind that behind the glitz and showmanship is an awful lot of hard work.

"We [television journalists] like to think of ourselves as big white-collar professionals and all that, but in reality, television is a lot like learning a trade," he says.

Bill makes it clear that you have to learn that trade from the ground up. You can learn a lot in school studying television journalism, but that is not all there is to it. Hands-on learning is the best training there is to prepare you for a job as a television journalist.

"Unless you are in a situation where you're around it almost constantly, you're just not going to learn a lot," he says.

"I used to see it all the time," he continues. "Kids think they can take an editing class their senior year in college and then put a tape together and go get a job, and it just doesn't happen. The people who get jobs in television are the ones who get hands-on experience. Sure, they'll do an internship, but then they'll do another internship. They stay with it."

In addition to experience working in the field, there are a variety of other qualities that Bill looks for when interviewing and hiring reporters, anchors, or producers. "What we tend to look for are people who seem to have a real passion for news. We look for people who are really well rounded. We try to find people who at least know what broadcast journalism is, whether it's through school or through an internship experience or whatever; people who know how to write and videotape."

There are three main areas Bill looks to when he is hiring reporters: how they sound, how they look, and how the quality of their writing comes across during a simulated broadcast on their demo tape. "Television, in a nutshell, kind of comes down to that," he says.

"It's very hard when you're starting out because you hate the sound of your voice. But you have to figure out a way to make your voice sound better to yourself and, therefore, better to other people as well. Same thing for your look, you know? And that's why it's so hard to get a television job without having done a whole lot of it, because everybody looks crummy their first time out. You just have to keep doing it over and over and over, until, with the help of others, you get to the level where you're a little bit more polished and professional in what you do."

Don't let yourself get discouraged, is Bill's message to all those who want to work in television news.

"Persistence means a lot," he says. "I think that certainly a big part of it is just knowing that, 'Hey, I'm up against 1,000 other people for one job, but if I really want that job, I'd better keep trying.'

"I've heard of people who were living at home for two years sending out tapes, working at whatever, and finally they got a good opportunity. So I think persistence is probably one of the biggest keys."

## MEET A SOUND AND LIGHTING TECHNICIAN

Stephen is a freelance sound and lighting technician who works out of a small town in New York—but far from New York City.

Much of his work involves shooting commercials, although he also has worked on videos and a program for the Discovery Channel, as well as on sporting events such as New York's Empire State Games and the international Goodwill Games. To augment his salary, he also works in theater lighting and sound.

Stephen has worked as everything from a gaffer and an electrician to a sound man. If a production has a small budget, as plenty of them in his market do, he sometimes ends up performing the tasks of all those positions during one shoot.

While many sound and lighting technicians in larger markets have the freedom to specialize in one area, he finds it easier to be a jack-of-all-trades. "In a market as small as this, if you're extremely specialized, in some ways it's the kiss of death," he notes.

Stephen—who before working as a sound and lighting technician installed car stereos for a living—didn't get into this field until he was in his thirties. Yet he always had been interested in electronics and related equipment.

"One of my strong points is that I'm extremely mechanically inclined," he says. "I'm curious about everything, and I have been all my life."

He earned an associate's degree in communications that he says helped teach him about photography and imaging. "That was where I got to fill in some of the pieces of the puzzle," he says. "It was a good foundation, but a lot of what I got there wasn't real-world experience."

To help him gain that practical experience, he took an internship with a local film company, working on industrial films and children's videos.

"The way I did it is I followed a guy around," he says. "And it wouldn't necessarily be the same guy, but anytime I was on a job, I followed somebody around and I watched what he did. And when he needed help, there I was, two feet behind him. After I followed people around long enough, I could start going out on my own and doing things because I knew what had to be done."

After the internship, when he was first starting out, Stephen did a lot of low-paying theater work and installed home-stereo systems on the side while he waited for film and television jobs to come his way.

"It took me a few years to build up to where I could get enough work at it to make a living," he says.

"You have to earn your reputation," he continues, "by doing good work and networking with people in the field. Perhaps just as important, however, is being someone who gets along well with others.

"Quite frankly, if people don't like you, even if your skill is good, it's going to limit the number of times you get hired," he states.

He says if employers in this field can choose between someone with excellent skills who is difficult and someone with lesser skills who is easy to get along with, they'll pick the second person every time.

Now, as an established freelancer, Stephen works fairly regularly, but his schedule is by no means set in stone.

"It varies tremendously," he says, when asked how many days a week he works, "from none to all of them. It's hard to come up with an average, but I'd say I work a couple of days a week—sometimes a lot more, and sometimes a lot less."

The freedom to pick and choose when he wants to work is a bonus, but that comes with strings attached. Stephen says there have been times when he has turned down work to go on vacation with his family, and then worried the whole time about how much not taking that job was costing him.

"If you try to plan stuff, you kind of pray nobody calls you when you planned it, so that you don't have to choose between going on vacation and taking the job," he says.

Also, because he is a freelancer and he does not have a union to watch out for him as Hollywood crews do, Stephen at times feels pressured by employers.

"So much of everything can be negotiated," he says. "You know, people are negotiating your rate, they're taking time out of your lunch. They're just really pushing you, physically pushing you to the limits of how fast you can move gear and get things set up."

When asked if he's happy with his career, he admits, "Sometimes I'm absolutely thrilled with it, and other times I hate it.

"Sometimes the jobs are so great I can't believe I'm getting paid for what I'm doing. I've been paid to fly in helicopters. I've been paid to jet-boat up the Niagara Gorge. Sometimes I like it just because it's an incredible learning experience. Sometimes I just like it because I'm outdoors, in nature. Sometimes it can just be because I'm driving around the country, seeing things that I like.

"And other times I can be trying to force myself awake while some corporate guy talks about corporate policy in a small office that's been heated up to 110 degrees by all the lights, and I've just eaten a big lunch and I'm just dying."

Overall, though, he says he's happy with his job and would recommend it as a career choice. His advice to those considering work in television light and sound would be to get an internship while in college, as he did.

Students can prepare for the field even earlier, he says, by choosing classes and extracurricular activities in high school that are in the field. He recommends working in your school's audio-visual department, or taking photography classes to learn the fundamentals of how light behaves. Another good move is to work with the theater department, not only on lights and sound, but also in set construction and carpentry.

"The more you know about the principles of light and the physics of sound, the better off you are," he says. "The more well rounded you are, the better employee it makes you. The more you understand what the other people are doing, the better you can interact with them to make things run smoothly and successfully."

# 8

# For Your Consideration

Now that you have learned a little more about the specific jobs to be had in television, you should take a few moments to consider some general truths about working in the television industry.

This chapter reviews some of the issues already raised in individual sections, such as location and competition. It also suggests some questions you might want to ask yourself. Included are a couple of pros and cons regarding a job in television, just to get you thinking some more.

## COMPETITION

One of the biggest considerations you need to be aware of before pursuing a career in television is that there is a lot of competition. For every position, particularly in the larger markets for television news and the network shows on the entertainment side, there are thousands of eager applicants. The supply exceeds the demand.

Are you up for some strong competition? Will you have the skills and persistence it is going to take to land a good job in television?

## LOCATION

Where you want to live and where you will best be able to find the job you want may be two different places.

For instance, if you want to be an actor in television, you will most likely have to move to Los Angeles because that's where virtually all of the entertainment shows are shot. While there are opportunities in other big cities, like New York—where most daytime serials, or soaps, are produced—your best bet in this instance is the West Coast.

Likewise, you might enjoy living in a small town but want to make it big in television news. Remember, the bigger the city, the bigger the market, and the bigger the paycheck.

Which type of career you wish to have in television, and the degree of success you have, in terms of money and fame, are directly related to location. Are you willing to make the move if it becomes necessary?

## EDUCATION

Pursuing an education after graduating from high school is an important step toward getting a good job anywhere, and that includes within the television industry. Sure, you can probably get a job as a production assistant or some other entry-level job in television and work your way up. Hands-on experience is important—even vital—but many employers want to see some kind of confirmation on paper that you know the business. That could mean a college diploma or some other kind of certificate specific to the job you are seeking. Are you willing to go on to college, or possibly to enroll in a trade school?

## AGENTS AND UNIONS

Several jobs in television require that you hire an agent, especially if you are on-air talent. Using their connections and business savvy, agents make getting work in television a lot easier. However, you also have to share the wealth with them and listen to their advice, even if you think you know your career better than they do.

Likewise, almost every position in television has to deal with unions in some form or another. Actors have the Screen Actors Guild and others, directors have the Directors Guild of America, and broadcast technicians are covered under the International Alliance of Theatrical and Stage Employees (which covers television as well).

Unions protect those who belong to them by making sure their members' pay, working conditions, and benefits are fair and reliable. In exchange for the support unions provide, you are required to pay dues, and you may be asked to participate in a strike if your union and those they are negotiating with cannot come to an agreement.

Can you give up some control over your career to agents and union representatives, or do you feel you need to call all the shots yourself?

## Paying Your Dues

Usually when you are first starting in your chosen field, you are going to have to perform some jobs that seem too easy or boring, or that don't challenge you or improve your skills. Even once you become somewhat established, you are most likely going to be called upon to pitch in and perform some tasks you don't particularly enjoy. This is especially true in the smaller markets because there are fewer people on the staff. Are you willing to pitch in and do whatever it takes to reach your goals?

## PROS AND CONS

**Pro: A job in television is exciting and glamorous.**

This statement is especially true if you are one of the people whose job requires you to be on the air. Television is a major form of fun and entertainment in America, and it holds a lot of influence. Being a part of that power, at any level, can be pretty exciting.

**Con: Although the glamour part is fun, jobs in television can also be a lot of hard work.**

We see the anchor or the reporter in front of the camera, delivering the news. What we don't see, and what we very rarely think about, is the hours these people spend off camera, researching stories, writing copy, and rehearsing, as well as the many years of hard work that led to their current positions.

It's easy to see or read interviews with celebrities on the entertainment side of television and think, "Man, they've got it made." Just remember, these people went on a lot of auditions and no doubt suffered a lot of rejection before they made a name for themselves.

Then there is the downside of glamour and fame. You can't go out in public without being recognized and bothered. Lots of times people expect you to be perfect, not only in connection to the quality of the job you do, but in your personal life, as well.

**Pro: Jobs in television pay well.**

Depending on which market you enter and the type of job you pursue, yes, you can make a lucrative salary with a career in television. Some positions, in larger markets for news and at the networks, can bring in salaries in the triple digits.

**Con: The pay is not always good.**

There are several jobs in broadcast television that pay well, but those are typically management positions or jobs associated with a hit television series. For the majority of jobs in television, the pay is generally low to average. This is especially true for entry-level positions.

A recent survey by Vernon Stone of the Missouri School of Journalism indicates that more than half of the people who work in broadcast news have thought about leaving the field because of low pay. This includes reporters, camera operators, and even producers who, in the smaller markets, can't even keep up with the basic cost of living.

On the entertainment side, keep in mind that the main union for television actors, the Screen Actors Guild, has found that the average yearly income its members earn from acting jobs is $5,000.

## NOW THAT YOU KNOW

Is a career in television right for you? After reading this book you are now aware of many of the career options available and how to get hired to perform them. You are also aware of some of the pros and cons regarding the pursuit of a television profession. Are you convinced that this is where you belong? If so, you are already well on your way. As you now know, determination and persistence are keys to success in this demanding yet rewarding field.

# Glossary

**affiliates**   The local stations that the large networks have agreements with to air their shows.

**apprentice**   Someone who is just beginning at a certain job. Apprentices learn from experienced professionals in their field, and they may perform easy tasks before being allowed to take on more responsibilities.

**best boy**   The second-in-command in charge of lighting technicians working on a television broadcast.

**commercial television**   Broadcast television that depends on the money brought in by commercial advertisers to keep running. Most of the broadcast television that we see today is commercial television.

**commission**   The percentage of money a sales representative makes on the amount he or she sells, or that an agent takes from a client's pay.

**demo tape**   A video portfolio of work performed by a person who is seeking on-camera work.

**dubbing**   Rerecording the voices of those on camera so that they are more clear, or inserting sounds for dramatic effect.

**editing bay**   The room in which an editor works.

**electronic news gathering (ENG)**   Refers to the video footage or satellite transmissions of television news crews.

**Federal Communications Commission (FCC)**
The organization that regulates and oversees broadcast television, as well as other communications entities.

**feed**  The programming signals that local affiliates tap into so that they can broadcast programs that the networks provide.

**gaffer**  The person in charge of lighting technicians working on a television broadcast.

**grips**  The people who work with equipment related to lighting that does not have cords attached. Grips also set up, maintain, and tear down the gear that removes, reflects, or otherwise manipulates the light.

**internship**  A job performed by a student or beginner to gain insight and experience in a field. These are usually unpaid positions, although some might offer a small salary.

**meteorologist**  Someone who has studied the weather. Meteorologists on television are also called weathercasters.

**noncommercial television**  Broadcasting that does not rely on commercial revenue, but on the generosity of the public.

**portfolio**  A collection of samples of a person's work.

**postproduction**  The time after a show has been shot, when it is cleaned up and finishing touches are added.

**preproduction**  The time leading up to a television show making it on the air.

**production**  When something is being filmed or videotaped, or, in the case of a live show, the time during which it is being broadcast.

**programming**   What shows the public sees, which day and what time they are aired, and how long they stay on the air.

**syndication**   The leasing of a television show after its initial run.

# For More Information

International Alliance of Theatrical Stage Employees, Moving Picture Technicians, Artists and Allied Crafts of the United States, Its Territories and Canada, AFL-CIO, CLC
General Office
1515 Broadway, Suite 601
New York, NY 10036
(212) 730-1770
Web site: http://www.iatse.lm.com/

## IN THE UNITED STATES
ABC (American Broadcasting Company)
http://www.abc.go.com

American Federation of Television and Radio Artists
5757 Wilshire Boulevard, 9th Floor
Los Angeles, CA 90036
(323) 634-8100
Web site: http://www.aftra.org

Broadcast Executive Directors Association (BEDA)
Web site: http://www.careerpage.org/joblist.htm

CBS
http://www.cbs.com

Directors Guild of America (DGA)
7920 Sunset Boulevard
Los Angeles, CA 90046
(310) 289-2000
Web site: http://www.dga.org

Federal Communications Commission (FCC)
445 12th Street SW
Washington, DC 20554
(202) 418-0190
(888) 225-5322
Web site: http://www.fcc.gov

Fox Television
3340 Ocean Boulevard, Suite 200
Santa Monica, CA 90405
(310) 314-9400
http://www.fox.com

NBC Studios (National Broadcasting Company)
3000 West Alameda Avenue
Burbank, CA 91523
(818) 840-4444
http://www.nbc.com

New York State Broadcasters Association, Inc.
1805 Western Avenue
Albany, NY 12203
(518) 456-8888
http://www.nysbroadcastersassn.org

Public Broadcasting Service (PBS)
http://www.pbs.org

Screen Actors Guild (SAG)
National Office
5757 Wilshire Boulevard
Los Angeles, CA 90036-3600
(323) 954-1600
Web site: http://www.sag.com

Society of Motion Picture and Television Engineers
    (SMPTE)
595 West Hartsdale Avenue
White Plains, NY 10607
(914) 761-1100
Web site: http://209.29.37.166/

Stuntmen's Association
10660 Riverside Drive, 2nd Floor, Suite E
Toluca Lake, CA 91602
(818) 766-4334
http://www.stuntmen.com

Stuntwomen's Association of Motion Pictures, Inc.
12457 Ventura Boulevard, Suite 208
Studio City, CA 91604
(888) 817-9267
http://www.stuntwomen.com

Writers Guild of America (WGA)
7000 West Third Street
Los Angeles, CA 90048
(800) 548-4532
(323) 951-4000
Web site: http://www.wga.org

## IN CANADA

Canadian Broadcasting Corporation (CBC)
Head Office
250 Lanark Avenue
P.O. Box 3220, Station "C"
Ottawa, ON K1Y 1E4
(613) 724-1200
Web site: http://cbc.ca

Canadian Film and Television Production Association
    (CFTPA)
151 Slater Street, Suite 605
Ottawa, ON K1P 5H3
(800) 565-7440
(613) 233-1444
Web site: http://www.cftpa.ca

North American Broadcasting Association (NABA)
P.O. Box 500, Station A
Toronto, ON M5W 1E6
(416) 598-9877
Web site: http://www.nabanet.com

# For Further Reading

Aisbett, Mark. *So You Wanna Be a Stuntman: The Official Stuntman's Guidebook*. Highlands, BC: Lifedrivers Inc., 1999.

Angell, Robert. *Getting into Films and Television: How to Find the Best Way In*. Philadelphia, PA: Trans-Atlantic Publications, 1997.

Clark, Elaine A. *There's Money Where Your Mouth Is: An Insider's Guide to a Career in Voice-overs*. New York: Watson-Guptill Publications, 1995

Davis, Gary. *Working at a TV Station*. Danbury, CT: Children's Press, 1998.

Farris, Linda G. *Television Careers: A Guide to Breaking and Entering*. Fairfax, CA: Buy the Book Enterprises, 1995.

Fox, Deborah. *People at Work in TV News*. Parsippany, NJ: Dillon Press, 1998.

Hurwitz, Ann. *Choosing A Career in Film, Television, or Video*. New York: Rosen Publishing Group, 1996.

J. G. Ferguson Publishing Company Staff. *Preparing for a Career in Radio and Television*. Chicago: J. G. Ferguson Publishing Co., 1998.

Lafferty, Peter. *Radio & Television*. Danbury, CT: Franklin Watts, Inc., 1998.

Lewis, M. K. *Your Film Acting Career: How to Break into the Movies and TV and Survive in Hollywood*. 4th ed. Santa Monica, CA: Gorham House Publishing, 1998.

Moody, Chip. *Moments: The Life and Career of a Texas Newsman*. Dallas, TX: Taylor Publishing Co., 1995

Noronha, Shonan. *Television and Video Careers*. Lincoln, IL: NTC Contemporary Publishing Co., 1998.

Reed, Maxine K., and Robert M. Reed. *Career Opportunities in Television, Cable, Video, and Multimedia*. New York: Facts on File, 1999.

Ritchie, Michael. *Please Stand By: A Prehistory of Television*. New York: Penguin USA, 1995.

Rogers, Lynne. *Working in Show Business: Behind-the-Scenes Careers in Theater, Film, and Television*. New York: Watson-Guptill Publications, 1997.

Simon, Mark. *Art Direction for Film and TV: The Craft and Your Career*. New York: Quite Specific Media Group, Ltd., 1998.

Sotnak, Lewann. *Director: Film, TV, Radio, and Stage*. Mankato, MN: Capstone Books, 2000.

Wake, Susan. *Advertising*. Ada, OK: Garrett Educational Corp., 1990.

Winship, Michael. *Television*. New York: Random House, Inc., 1988.

Wordsworth, Louise. *Film and Television*. Chatham, NJ: Raintree Steck-Vaughn Publishers, 1999.

# Index

## T

Tarleton, Robert, 8
technicians, 14, 32, 36,
    49, 56–69, 95,
    98–102, 105
  schools for, 62–63
television
  commercial, 6, 7, 9,
    11, 52, 63
  history of, 3–6, 8, 12
  noncommercial/public,
    6, 7–8, 11, 63
theater, school or
    amateur, 18, 19,
    32, 51, 60, 62, 72,
    84, 89, 94, 95, 98,
    99, 101
traffic, 48
transmission operators,
    58

## U

unions, 17, 20, 46, 94,
    104–105, 107

## V

video control engineers, 57
videotape engineers, 57
visual/graphic artists, 80–84

## W

Walson, John, 8
weathercasters/meteorolo-
    gists, 24, 28
writers, 13, 14, 31, 33,
    37–41, 64, 70,
    88–91
writing, 21, 22, 23, 32,
    34, 87, 89, 97

## Z

Zworykin, Vladimir, 5